"I Forgive You, But..."

3 Steps That Can Heal Your Heart Forever!

Karen Jensen Salisbury

2 3 4 5 6 7 8 / 23 22 21 20 19

"I Forgive You, But . . . "
Copyright © 2017 by Karen Jensen Salisbury

ISBN: 978-168031-131-0

Published by Harrison House Publishers
www.harrisonhouse.com

Endorsements for "I Forgive You, But..."

If you've been hurt, the stories and scriptures you'll read here can help your heart to heal through the power of forgiveness. Karen writes with compassion and clarity. I highly recommend this book.

-**Lynne Hammond**, Pastor, Living Word Christian Center,
Brooklyn Park, Minnesota
Author of *Devotions for the Praying Heart* and *The Master is Calling*
lynnehammond.org

I am happy to recommend another fabulous book about real life issues by my friend, Karen Jensen Salisbury! We all need help forgiving when someone does us wrong. This book tells you how to do it, with inspiring personal stories and easy-to-understand biblical truths. Karen's open and engaging writing style makes this a life-changing read. Everyone needs this book!

-**Beth Jones**, Pastor, Valley Family Church, Kalamazoo, Michigan
Author of *The Basics with Beth*
thebasicswithbeth.com

Forgiveness is one of the most powerful and under-used forces on the face of the earth. It can unlock the doors of the penitentiary of the past where the chains of bitterness keep you from making progress in every area of your life. In her latest work, Karen Jensen Salisbury has captured the true essence of this very personal issue. *"I Forgive You, But . . ."* is a must-read for all those who need to be set free.

-**Matt & Kendal Hagee**, Pastors, Cornerstone Church
Hosts of *The Difference* show
gettv.org/TheDifference

Karen is definitely qualified to write on this vitally important topic of forgiveness, and I recommend this book highly. Learning to walk in forgiveness will release you from emotional baggage, physical maladies, and introduce you to an abundant joy.

-**Rachel Burchfield**, President, Texas Bible Institute
Author of *Miracle Moments*
burchfield.org

Have you ever been wounded by someone who should know better? You are in good company. Countless people have been hurt, and millions more are suffering from the debilitating effects of harboring bitterness and resentment. In this powerful book, Karen Jensen Salisbury takes the reader on a powerful journey of hope, healing, and recovery. You don't have to remain "stuck" — instead, you can live a life of freedom and victory. Apply the powerful nuggets of truth found in this work in live your best life NOW!

-**Dr. Kynan Bridges**, Pastor, Grace & Peace Church, Tampa, Florida
Author of *Unmasking The Accuser* and *The Power of Prophetic Prayer*
kynanbridges.com

I love Karen's heart to give people knowledge on how to live the God kind of life. This book will show you how to forgive people and keep you in a great place to live in peace and happiness. It will change your life!

-**Sandy Scheer**, Pastor, Guts Church, Tulsa, Oklahoma
gutschurch.com

Karen is one of the happiest, emotionally healthiest, and wisest women I know. She writes from both years of helping others, as well as overcoming her own painful life-challenges. *"I Forgive You, But . . ."* is an insightful, inspiring, yet practical read that includes helpful action steps to guide you to your own freedom from emotional pain! I highly recommend it!

-**Rev. Matthew Beemer**, International Director, Club 1040
CLUB1040.com

Sometimes it's hard to forgive. We want someone to know how badly they've hurt us, or we want to see them suffer like we've suffered. But God wants to help us to let go of the pain — and it happens through the power of forgiveness. Karen tells us not only that we *should* forgive, but *why* we should and most importantly *how* to do it. You will be tremendously helped by this book and it can change your life!

-**Kate McVeigh**, President and Founder, Kate McVeigh Ministries
Author of *Get Over It* and *The Blessing of Favor*
katemcveigh.org

There is no greater harm to your life than unforgiveness. This book is filled with the applicable wisdom you need in order to forgive. We've known Karen for many years, and she has a wealth of information and first-hand experience as a wife, mother, pastor, Bible school instructor, and advisor to ministers. The knowledge in this much-needed book will arm you with the tools you need to overcome the deadliness of unforgiveness and walk away free!

-**Rod & Rebecca Sundholm**, Pastors, New Creation Church,
Hillsboro, Oregon
newcreationchurch.tv

It's hard to move forward after being wounded, but not forgiving someone does more damage to you than to the person that did the hurting. Many of us don't even know where to begin to forgive someone. In Karen's new book *"I Forgive You, But . . ."* you will find the tools to help you to move past the pain so you can step into your purpose. This book will help you discern the root of your unforgiveness and challenge you to not remain the same.

-**Janet Boynes**, President and Founder, Janet Boynes Ministries
Author of *Called Out* and *Arise*
janetboynesministries.com

Has something ever happened in your life that's left you feeling so hurt, you've struggled with forgiving the person? We can all use help at those times, and this book does just that! It gives us the tools to help put the anger, feeling of betrayal, or emotional pain we're feeling behind us through the power of forgiveness. Karen's unique way of sharing real-life stories, along with biblical principles, helps us take steps forward to forgive and finally be set free. We know you'll be so glad you made the time to read this book!

-**Tim & Renee Burt**, Tim & Renee Burt Ministries,
Minneapolis, Minnesota
readfreshmanna.blogspot.com

Heartbreak can come in like a thief. It can steal the breath from your lungs, strip your last ounce of hope and withdraw you into dark places you never saw yourself. If that's you, then a book on forgiveness may be the last book you want to invest your time in. However, with a combination of practicality and Biblical instructions Karen lovingly walks you through action thoughts like, "It's okay to forgive and stay away," which leaves you more capable, stronger and freer.

-**Jamie Jones**, Speaker and Author of *Rich For Good*
jamiejones.org

This is a real, practical, helpful, in-your-face, powerful, we-need-to-talk-about-this-NOW kind of book! You will need to keep it by your bedside to reference at a moment's notice. The scriptures and declarations in Step 2 are pure gold. Karen takes a 360-degree look at forgiveness, digging down deep to the root issues, what unforgiveness looks like, our struggles with it, how we should deal with it and how to use God's Word to get results. These truth-filled, hope-filled pages will breathe life into your hurting heart.

-**Amy Schafer**, Pastor, Grace Life Church, Pittsburgh, Pennsylvania
Host, "Real Life" at Cornerstone Network
gracelifechurch.tv

I'm so glad that Karen has undertaken the task of addressing this monumental issue of forgiveness. Karen is an outstanding writer, and true to form, she illuminates this subject with scriptural insights and helpful application. For too long, people have labored under the heavy yoke of unforgiveness, often due to misunderstandings and misconceptions that cause them to either suppress their feelings or be governed by them. This book will introduce you to the freedom and liberty that God has for each one of us.

-**Tony Cooke**, Bible Teacher, Tony Cooke Ministries
Author of *Grace: The DNA of God* and *In Search of Timothy*
tonycooke.org

Contents

Introduction

You might have picked up this book because the title applies to your life. You might have someone in mind and you're saying, "I forgive you, but . . . ."

Maybe you've tried to forgive, but you just couldn't.

Maybe you thought you forgave, but what happened just keeps coming back, and it feels so raw and painful, you wonder if you've failed in the forgiveness department.

Maybe you know you *should* forgive, but you're just plain mad, and you don't want to forgive.

Or maybe you've forgiven the same person again and again, and you don't want to do it anymore.

Here are just a few of the things I've heard (or even felt) that complete the sentence, *I forgive you, but . . .*

• you don't deserve it.

• I won't forget!

• I want you to be sorry.

• I still hate you.

• I don't want you to get away with it.

• I want you to admit you were wrong.

• I want you to understand the pain you've caused.

• someone has to pay.

• I want you to know how much you hurt me.

• I don't want you to be blessed.

• it's hard.

If any of those thoughts are your thoughts (or some variation thereof), then this book is for you. We're going to look at those thoughts and feelings, and see what God has to say about them. Because at the end of the day, what God wants for you is *freedom and peace and blessing,* and forgiveness is the way to get you there.

At the end of the day, what God wants for you is freedom and peace.

You *know* you should forgive, right? You may have even given it your best shot. Maybe you've given it lip service and said, "Yeah, yeah, I forgive them," but deep inside you're not buying it. You've tried and yet failed to forgive. Every time that person's name (or that situation) comes up, the vein stands out in your neck, or the pain punches you in the stomach. Thoughts of what happened still swirl in your head in the wee hours of the night, making you toss and turn in your bed and lose sleep.

Maybe you still get that "rot gut" feeling every time something reminds you. Or maybe you're just holding onto unforgiveness on purpose to teach them a lesson.

You may have taken a shot at forgiveness, but you know you're not totally free.

Have You Been Hurt?

Most of us Christians know that we're supposed to forgive, right? We know from the Bible and years of sermons that we're not supposed to hold a grudge.

Let's say, for example, that someone has done you wrong, and you're very upset about it. You've told a few friends, and if the name of the person comes up in conversation, you get that horrible feeling in the pit of your stomach. But if I were to ask you, "Are you harboring unforgiveness against that person?" your good Christian answer would be, "Oh no, I forgive them" because you know you're supposed to say that.

I've learned over the years not to ask that question anymore because I always get that same answer when it's plain to see that it's still very much an issue. People just don't *know* that they're still holding a grudge (and therefore they're not free from it).

So let me ask it this way: "Have you been hurt?"

I think we can all answer "yes!" to that question. I think anyone who's been alive longer than about 15 minutes has been hurt. Sadly, it's part of life in this world.

First, let me say I'm so sorry. I know your pain is real. You may think, "No one understands what I've gone through" (and that's true) and "How can I forgive the horrible things I've endured, the wounds and scars I wear every day?"

I haven't walked in your shoes, and I don't know exactly what has happened to you. But I have walked through some painful things, and I've walked through some painful things with other people.

Maybe your hurt came when someone wounded you in terrible ways, even tried to destroy you. Maybe you counted on someone and they let you down horribly, or you were stunned when someone you trusted just totally betrayed you. Maybe it was even a Christian, who should've known better! Maybe someone stole from you or was just plain rotten to you.

You may have suffered with unforgiveness for a long time. Maybe something happened to you long ago and, in spite of your efforts to forgive, you haven't been able to let it go all the way. Or maybe it's something recent, but the hurt goes so deep, you can't see your way to forgive. These are all very real, very painful realities.

In today's world, it seems there are a lot of good reasons to harbor a grudge. It's also a very socially acceptable concept to retaliate against those who have hurt us — revenge is a very popular theme for movies, books, TV, and news. But revenge is not God's way. His wish — and mine too — is freedom from the hurt, so you can have peace in your heart and mind. We want you to have freedom to move past the pain, and forgiveness is the way to get there.

....

God's wish for you is freedom from the hurt,
so you can have peace.

....

I want you to discover what I have about the power of forgiveness. Too many are walking around wounded or angry or even sick from the hurts of the past while God has the answer. It might not seem like it, but the answer is forgiveness. I've seen *miracles* happen when people forgive! And I want you to know about them, so they can happen in your life too.

There are stories in this book about people like you, people who have tried to forgive or thought they forgave or who didn't want to forgive. But once they truly forgave, God was able to do great things in their lives!

Maybe you don't want to forgive — you want people to get what they deserve!

I understand. I really do. Sometimes this world is a hard, hard place, and hurts come from other people, from situations and things beyond our control, from horrible circumstances and violated expectations. But God wants you to be free from the hurt, and that's what this book is about.

It's Not Okay to Stay Hurt

While it's fairly normal to *get* hurt as a Christian human being on planet Earth, it's not okay to *stay* hurt. God doesn't want that for you! In fact, can I put it to you in fairly harsh terms? Staying hurt is really harboring unforgiveness.

....

Staying hurt is really harboring unforgiveness.

....

I know, I know! That's a mean thing to say! Ouch! And you might be thinking, "Oh no, I'm not harboring unforgiveness, Karen. I know better than that." Or you might even be thinking, "But you don't know what they did to me!"

And of course, you're right, I don't know. I haven't felt your particular pain. But one thing I know for sure is that I don't want you to have to live with it a moment longer, and neither does God. He loves you! And he sent his Son, Jesus, to bear those pains for you, and to set you free.

When someone has done something hurtful or stupid or mean or ignorant to you and it's affected your life, it just doesn't seem like it's possible to forgive them, especially when you're living with the results. But here's what I've learned: if you forgive, you can come out of it. When you choose to forgive, you're choosing God's way of acting and reacting, and that means you're choosing to let him take over in the situation. Not only does forgiveness make your pain go away, but it allows God to move.

Don't live a moment longer with the wrongs that others have done to you or with your own regrets and failures. You can't hold onto the past and walk into the future God has for you! Today is a new day — a day to let it go and walk in freedom. We all have opportunities to hold onto things that have happened to us. I don't know about you, but I don't want to let what others do to me determine how I live. Unforgiveness only perpetuates pain, both in my life and the lives of those around me.

Unforgiveness only perpetuates pain,
both in my life and the lives of those around me.

Not only can it poison my life, but it can poison my family, friends, and loved ones. If I refuse to forgive, I hurt myself *and* those around me. Let's face it, hurt people can end up hurting people! Bitter people are no fun to be around. They can't sleep. They get ulcers. They're grumpy. They start to see only the negative in every situation because their life is filled with these feelings of resentment and anger.

My friend, if you choose to hold on to bitterness, you can lose your peace, your joy, your friends, your family, and possibly even your health. It's just not worth it. When you refuse to forgive, you may feel like you're punishing the other person, but the only person paying the price is you and those around you. But through forgiveness, God can bring you into a future that is far better than you can even imagine!

In This Book

So are you ready for peace and freedom? Are you ready to move past the pain and walk into your bright future? Are you ready to accept the challenge to forgive? Don't cheat yourself out of a life of freedom and joy. The future God has planned for you is much better than your past.

God is saying to you *today*, "Let it go. Forgive them their debts, just as I have forgiven yours."

In my own life, I've learned the power of forgiveness — both for myself and the many, many people I've ministered to. Miracles happen when we forgive!

Miracles happen when we forgive!

God wants you to be free from hurt, and so do I. It's what Jesus came for! Galatians 5:1 (NIV) says, "It is for freedom that Christ has set us free. Stand firm, then, and do not let yourselves be burdened again by a yoke of slavery." There is freedom in forgiveness! Jesus doesn't want you to be a slave to hurts for another moment.

It might feel impossible to forgive right now, but I invite you to read through the book. You've already taken the first step of the journey by reading this far. Hurray for you! Now keep going. By bathing your spirit in the truths of God's Word in this book, you can cut the chains of past hurts and walk away free.

We're going to go at it in three steps. I truly believe that following these steps can heal your heart forever!

Step 1: Read this. This section contains stories of people who have also been hurt in their lives and how they found freedom through forgiveness (the names have been changed, but the stories are real). I believe that as you read their stories, you will receive the faith to forgive too.

Step 2: Meditate and declare this. In this section, the scriptures from step 1 are all written out, along with declarations that enable you to take hold of the Word for yourself and apply it to your own life. Here you can bathe your spirit in what God says about forgiveness, and you can return to it as often as needed.

Step 3: Do this. This is the "doing" part of forgiveness, where you'll write down the name(s) of those you need to forgive and date it. This will be the proof you can point to, the reinforcement of your commitment to forgive that will stand the test of time.

In my experience as a pastor and Bible school instructor, I've gone through this process with a lot of people and have seen miraculous things happen. As they forgive, they walk into their future free from hurts of the past. I believe that can happen for you too! This book will give you the tools to overcome anything that has come against you or caused you pain.

You have what it takes, so *keep reading*. You can be free! Soak your spirit in these truths from God's Word about forgiveness, follow the three steps outlined in this book, and you can get there.

Here we go.

STEP 1

Read This

Chapter 1

Life Is So Unfair

Barbara's Story: I first met Barbara when she came to church on a Sunday morning. She came not long after my husband, the founding pastor, had unexpectedly died, and I had taken over his job pastoring the church, so I was pretty new at it. (You can read more about that story in my book, *Why God Why? What To Do When Life Doesn't Make Sense.*)

Barbara caught my eye because she seemed so unhappy. I would even use the word downtrodden. Her shoulders were hunched over, she didn't make eye contact with anyone, and she looked as if she would cry at any moment. She had three children, all under seven years of age, and none of them looked like each other.

When I greeted her on her way out the door, she looked down as I shook her hand. She murmured "thank you," then walked toward the parking lot. I wanted to speak with her longer, but the line of people behind her waiting to shake my hand consumed my attention, and she slipped quietly away.

It was about her third Sunday when I finally managed to catch her off to the side for a quick conversation, and was able to ask, "Is there anything I can do for you?" For the first time she looked into my eyes, as if to see if I really meant it, then looked quickly away. She started to shake her head, but somehow mustered up the courage to look back at me and softly say, "Could I meet with you sometime?"

I could tell it was a brave step for her. Of course I agreed, and we set up a time to meet.

Beaten Down and Wounded

On the day of our meeting, Barbara was dry-eyed and matter-of-fact as she spelled out a horrifying childhood. From the time she was two or three years old, she had been abused both physically and emotionally by several male members of her family.

As a result, her adult life was a mess. Her three children had three different fathers, and none of the men had stayed with her. Now she was struggling not only to raise three children on her own but to form any kind of relationship with anyone, even friends and coworkers.

If you heard her whole story, you would understand why. She had no kind of normalcy in her past, no way of knowing how to engage with people in a healthy way, and it affected every area of her life. She was so beaten down and wounded and afraid. My heart broke for her.

After meeting with her several times, I was in my prayer closet at home one night, praying for her. I cried out to the Lord, "Father, this is so unfair! It's not Barbara's fault that she was born into this family that abused her, yet her life is a mess because of what those horrible people did to her. How can I help her? It can't be hopeless. You are the great equalizer. Is there an answer for her?"

And the Lord said, "Yes, there's an answer for her."

I was excited! Yay God! I said, "I knew it! What's the answer for this precious woman?"

I was totally surprised by his answer. He said, "Forgiveness."

That stopped me short. It wasn't what I was expecting at all. I said, "No way! Are you sure, Lord? It doesn't seem like forgiveness will help her get over everything that's happened to her."

And right then, the Lord told me something that I've never forgotten. He said, "Forgiveness is how my relationship started with you."

God said, "Forgiveness is how my relationship started with you."

Wow! That was huge! When the Lord spoke that to my heart, I realized there was way more to forgiveness than I had thought. Every one of us started our relationship with God with forgiveness. Colossians 2:13 says, "When you were dead in your transgressions and the uncircumcision of your flesh, He made you alive together with Him, having forgiven us all our transgressions" (NASB).

Think about it. God made us alive together with him by forgiving us. You could say that forgiveness is God's way of making a fresh start, his way of executing do-overs. After all, it's how he started *you* and *me* over again. He made us new creatures in Christ, where old things passed away and all things became new (2 Cor. 5:17). He transformed us into brand new, born-again, righteous beings by *forgiving* us.

Always Our Choice

So Barbara and I embarked on a journey to study the Bible about forgiveness. Because most of us can't forgive on our own, we need supernatural help! And God's Word is where we get it.

First, I asked Barbara if she was born again, if she had received Jesus as her Lord and Savior. If she hadn't yet done that, she would be outside of God's covenant family and wouldn't understand anything from the Bible. (If that's you, and you haven't yet received Jesus as your Lord and Savior, you can do so right now by turning to page 175 and praying that prayer. It will be the best thing you've ever done in your life, and will open up all of God's blessings to you. If you haven't received Jesus yet, go there now, then come back and resume reading here).

Barbara assured me that she was born again, so we dove into the Word and we discovered that God has a *lot* to say about forgiveness. It's his go-to reaction with human beings. His very nature is forgiveness!

As Barbara and I studied, we found that God's way of dealing with mankind is forgiveness. In Isaiah 43:25, he says, "I, even I, am He who blots out your transgressions for My own sake; and I will not remember your sins." God never has unforgiveness in his relationship with you. Never.

> *God never has unforgiveness in his relationship with you. Never.*

The good news is that as born-again Christians, we have God's very nature inside of us, so we've not only been forgiven, we also totally have the capacity to forgive. We just need supernatural help to do it! Thankfully, we have supernatural help. As we soak our spirits in the truth of God's Word on forgiveness, it gives us the strength we need to choose to do things God's way.

But even though we have supernatural help, it will always be our choice to forgive. God has created us with a will of our own, and he allows us to choose as we will. In the book of Deuteronomy he says, "I call heaven and earth as witnesses today against you, that I have set before you life and death, blessing and cursing; therefore choose life, that both you and your descendants may live" (30:19). He does give us a clue in this verse when he says, "Choose life!" But it's always our choice.

Later, we see Joshua exercising his own right to choose when he said, "Choose you this day whom ye will serve . . . but as for me and my house, we will serve the Lord" (Joshua 24:15).

God won't ever *make* you forgive. No one can make you; it has to be your choice. The good news is that he's standing by, ready to help you do it. He just wants you to *want to* forgive. When you take it to him and ask for his help, he's right there with his supernatural help to put you over.

Your Blessing Pipe

The more Barbara and I studied, the more we learned that forgiveness is how God deals with mankind. He is not a grudge-holder. He is a forgiving father. Since you are his child, you should (and can!) also be a forgiver. It's for your ultimate benefit. Harboring unforgiveness is like drinking poison and expecting the other person to die; it's not hurting the one you're holding a grudge against, it's hurting *you*.

Harboring unforgiveness is like drinking poison and expecting the other person to die.

Unforgiveness is going against God's principles. I came to realize that if I don't choose to deal with people in the same manner God does (by forgiving), then I'm disobeying his many admonitions to forgive and I'm outside of his realm, so I can expect the result of that in my life. I can't go against his nature (by harboring unforgiveness) and expect his blessings to flow to me.

I like to say it this way: If we harbor unforgiveness, we're "clogging the blessing pipe." All of God's blessings belong to and are always flowing to us in Christ Jesus (Eph. 1:3), and he *always* loves us (Jer. 31:3). But when we disobey his many commands to forgive, that clogs the pipe. There is something standing between us and all of his blessings, and that thing is unforgiveness. Unforgiveness puts us outside of his promises.

On the other hand, when we *do* choose to forgive, we're right there in his *bailiwick*. I know *bailiwick* is a funny word, but Merriam-Webster's dictionary defines it as "a special domain" or "a jurisdiction." When we choose forgiveness, we're right there with God in his domain; we're in his jurisdiction, which means all that he is and all that he's promised is available to us. You could say he lives in "forgiveness land" where forgiveness is the way of life.

But if we choose to hold a grudge or keep unforgiveness, then we're *outside* of his jurisdiction, out of the reach of his blessings and protection. I don't want to be there, do you?

I'm glad to live in God's domain and receive his blessings all the time. I've discovered that one of the requirements for living there is that I must also forgive, as he does. Ephesians 4:32 says it this way: "Be kind to one another, tenderhearted, forgiving one another, just as God in Christ also forgave you." So I've decided (and I hope you do too) that I don't want to live in "grudge-holding land" because God's not there! I want to choose forgiveness, and keep my blessing pipe clear.

Do You Need to Forgive God?

Let's just be honest. Some of us need to forgive God. When something bad has happened in our lives, or something didn't happen the way we wanted or expected, it's easy to blame God. It's easy to say things like, "How could God let this happen? Where was God in all of this? I prayed but he didn't answer."

But I'm here to tell you God is not your enemy. All of his intentions and actions toward you are *always* good and *never* bad. First John 1:5 says that "God is light and in Him is no darkness at all," and James 1:17 says, "Every good gift and every perfect gift is from above, and comes down from the Father of lights, with whom there is no variation or shadow of turning."

....

All of his intentions and actions toward you
are always good and never bad.

....

God is only good, and his mercy endures forever (Ps. 118). He doesn't change back and forth from good to bad, sometimes blessing and sometimes cursing. You can trust him (Prov. 3:5–6) because he always has your best interest at heart. So don't hold any anger or malice in your heart toward him. Just get it out in the open, tell him how you feel, and let it go.

The devil would love for you to believe that the bad stuff that may have happened in your life is God's fault. Or at the very least, that he *allowed* it. The devil wants you to think that God doesn't care about you or he's mad at you or he's just not paying attention. He knows that if you're mad at God, he's got you right where he wants you — separated from your only help!

When my first husband died at 37 years of age, his sudden death left me parent to two teenaged sons and pastor to our four-year-old church. At the time, people said to me, "Oh Karen, you're so brave to keep holding onto God after something so devastating has happened." I guess they meant that *they* might be mad at God over such a thing (and really, that's just unforgiveness, isn't it?).

But my thought was, "This is no time to let go of God, not when I need him so much!" I knew I needed his help to get over the death of my husband, pastor a church by myself, and raise two boys through their teenaged years. It didn't make any sense to me to turn my back on the One who could help me!

Besides, I knew that it wasn't God who "took" my husband. My Heavenly Father is a good and loving Father, who wants only the best for his children. Sometimes people get confused about this, and they attribute terrible, evil things to God when really all evil comes from the devil.

There's an easy way to tell if something came from God or if it came from the devil. In John 10:10, Jesus says, "The thief does not come except to steal, and to kill, and to destroy. I have come that they may have life, and that they may have it more abundantly."

That's pretty black and white, isn't it? If there is stealing, killing, or destroying going on, it is the devil's doing, not God's.

Know Your Enemy

When we're harboring unforgiveness, we're dealing with hurts in a fleshly way instead of a spiritual way. And unfortunately, that's not the way to get healed of hurts. It just perpetuates them. But God wants to help you *overcome* the hurt, and that's done in the spirit, not the flesh.

Romans 8:13 says if we live according to the flesh we will die, but if we live by the Spirit we put the deeds of the flesh to death and we can live God's abundant life. That's a better way to live!

You could say it this way: flesh wants justification and judgment, but the spirit calls for mercy and forgiveness. It's so important to remember that we have an enemy in this earth, Satan, who wants us to live in the lower realm of the flesh. He doesn't want God's blessings to flow to us! So he sows as many seeds of division, strife and unforgiveness into our lives as he can, to clog our blessing pipe. You don't have to allow it! You can rise above it when you remember who your enemy is. It's not people, even though it looks like it.

Read that again: people are not your enemy, even though it looks like they are! Ephesians 6:12 says, "For we do not wrestle against flesh and blood, but against principalities, against powers, against the rulers of the darkness of this age, against spiritual hosts of wickedness in the heavenly places."

People are not your enemy,
even though it looks like they are!

When a person hurts you, don't wrestle with *them* (flesh and blood). Recognize where that spirit of strife, division, destruction and offense is coming from, and take authority over the devil! So many things that come against us (and would love to lodge in our hearts as unforgiveness) are simply a plot of the devil trying to distract us, trying to clog our blessing pipe. The devil hates us, and certainly doesn't want us walking in the blessings or in our calling, or in being a witness and examples to others.

And he's sneaky. He doesn't come marching up to you with a pitchfork and say, "I'm bringing trouble!" No, he uses people and situations to distract and torment you. Many times we forget that, or we don't recognize where the trouble is coming from, so we don't use our authority over the devil and overcome his tactics in the spirit realm. Instead we just react in the flesh by wanting to retaliate, or by attacking the person, or by holding a grudge.

One minister says it this way: "The biggest enemy of faith is unforgiveness." We see where it can affect so many areas of our lives! Let it not be said of us that we let down our faith by harboring unforgiveness. No, we're going to be smarter than that and recognize when the devil is trying to undermine our faith.

The apostle Paul talks about this in 2 Corinthians 2: "Now whom you forgive anything, I also forgive . . . lest Satan should take advantage of us; for we are not ignorant of his devices" (vv. 10–11). Let's not let the devil take advantage of us. We are not ignorant of his devices! We recognize when he's trying to distract us and undermine our faith through unforgiveness. So we turn the tables on him by forgiving.

When I was a pastor, I used to tell my congregation, "If you spot him, you got him!" Once you recognize that the real problem is the devil, you win! He only wins through deception. He can't overpower you because *you* are the one with all the power (Luke 10:19). He can only trick you into thinking he's winning. I often say, "Oh no you don't devil, I see you! So I resist you in Jesus' name and you must flee from me" (see James 4:7).

If you spot him, you got him!

When you feel hurt or angry at someone or things are going wrong in your life, or you're mad at God over it, stop and remember where all that trouble is coming from. The devil wants you focusing on hurts and disappointments so you don't remember who you are, why you're here, and what you're called to do. He's the king of distractions! Forgiveness is the spiritual reaction; it's one of the best ways to stop him in his tracks and derail his evil intentions.

The book of Luke gives us a good picture of what a non-carnal, forgiving Christian looks like:

But love your enemies, do good, and lend, hoping for nothing in return; and your reward will be great, and you will be sons of the Most High. For He is kind to the unthankful and evil. Therefore be merciful, just as your Father also is merciful. Judge not, and you shall not be judged. Condemn not, and you shall not be condemned. Forgive, and you will be forgiven.

Luke 6:35–37

Simple, right? Just love your enemies, do good, lend and look for nothing in return, be merciful, don't judge, don't condemn, and forgive! Okay, it may not seem simple, but if it's in the Bible, then it's possible for us to live like this! These are God's instructions for our lives, and if we're willing to live by them, he's more than willing to help us do it. He's not asking us to try to be perfect. He's asking us to let him live through us. I can do that! You can too.

A Remarkable Transformation

After a couple months of studying God's Word and feeding on forgiveness scriptures, Barbara and I sat down with her notebook and wrote down the names of the people she needed to forgive — those who had hurt and abused her so badly in the past. You'll be doing that, too, in step 3 (but don't get ahead of yourself! Read Steps 1 and 2 first, and give the Word time to soak into your spirit.)

It wasn't anything she could have done without the truths of God's Word deep in her heart and mind.

I wish you could have seen Barbara when this was all said and done! When she forgave all those people in her past for the horrible things that had happened to her in her childhood, her life changed. She was able to receive God's love. She then had the capacity to love people around her, including her children, family members, and fellow church members, and she was able to mend relationships.

It even affected her physical appearance. Her face looked lighter! She went from being a woman beaten down, sick, and perpetually discouraged to one who could laugh, enjoy relationships, and be healthy. The transformation was remarkable. It was one of the most satisfying things I have ever seen in ministry. God did a miracle in her life through the power of forgiveness!

As for me, I learned that forgiveness is the way to cut the chains of a painful past and become free. Since then, I've seen it happen again and again. I believe it will happen for you, too.

"I Forgive You, But You Don't Deserve It!"

I think that very often we think of forgiving as an *option*; "I'll forgive them if I feel like it and only if they *deserve* to be forgiven." But if that were the case, then none of the horrible people who abused Barbara as a child would have been (or should have been) forgiven. They didn't deserve it at all. But forgiving and deserving don't have anything to do with each other. We forgive because God says to and because he forgave us and because it sets us free. Period.

Really, forgiveness doesn't have anything at all to do with the person we're forgiving.

Forgiveness doesn't have anything at all to do with the person we're forgiving.

We don't forgive based on what they have or haven't done; we forgive because God says to and because it's our path to freedom. It's how we keep our blessing pipe unclogged!

After all, God forgave us when we didn't deserve it. Romans 5:8 says, "But God demonstrates His own love toward us, in that while we were still sinners, Christ died for us." While we were sinners, Jesus chose to die for us and pay for all our sins. He forgave us when we least deserved it. So doesn't it make sense that we are to forgive people when they don't deserve it?

God forgave us in Jesus because he is good, not because we are good. Aren't you *glad* that he didn't view forgiveness as an option but rather as part of his covenant? I am grateful every day for his forgiveness. It's not based on how I behave but on his determination to love at all costs.

It's the same for us. We forgive because God is good and he's in us, not because the person we're forgiving is good (or deserves it). Colossians 3:13 says, "Even as Christ forgave you, so you also must do." Christ forgave us without strings attached, out of his great mercy and love. Since he did, notice that verse says we *must* do it too! That doesn't sound like an option to me — it sounds like a commandment.

And we know that when we obey the Lord's commandments, things go well with us. Loving God means keeping his commandments. First John 5:3 says, "Loving God means doing what he tells us to do, and really, that isn't hard at all" (TLB). I'm so glad the Bible says it's not hard. That way, when it *feels* hard, I can remind myself that God says it isn't! I can choose to believe his Word.

Obeying God — in this case, choosing to forgive — is our path to freedom. It's not hard and we can do it! Jesus showed us the way.

We should be very glad that forgiveness has nothing to do with deserving because neither you nor I deserved to be forgiven. We were all the same before Jesus saved us. We were undeserving sinners. I'm just glad every day that God forgave me before I ever deserved it!

Be careful of wanting people to get what they deserve. I used to tell my students, "Be careful about using the 'D' word" (deserving). If you and I got what we deserve, we'd all die and go to hell." Thankfully, God's amazing covenant, bought by the blood of the Lamb, has delivered us when we didn't deserve it at all.

Cutting the Chain

The best analogy I can come up with for unforgiveness — or holding onto hurt — is that it's like attaching a ball and chain to your ankle. Every time you try to run your race, that ball *bang*s against your leg, hindering your progress and causing you pain. It affects every area of your life and steals your joy. It's bondage!

Hebrews 12:1 says, "Let us lay aside every weight, and the sin which so easily ensnares us, and let us run with endurance the race that is set before us." I truly believe that, among other things, unforgiveness is one of those weights and yes, one of those sins. It weighs us down! Every time you rehearse that pain, remember that wrong, feel that "rot gut" in your stomach, there's that ball and chain again, banging against your leg, keeping you from effectively running your race.

The only way I know to cut that chain and run unhindered into your future with peace and freedom, is to forgive.

The only way I know to cut the chain and run unhindered into your future with peace and freedom, is to forgive.

The Bible points this out so clearly in Mark 11. Some of us recognize verses 23 and 24 as great "faith" verses, all about speaking to the mountain of trouble and casting it into the sea; about having what you say, and believing you receive when you pray (before you actually see it come to pass).

> **For assuredly, I say to you, whoever says to this mountain, 'Be removed and be cast into the sea,' and does not doubt in his heart, but believes that those things he says will be done, he will have whatever he says. ²⁴ Therefore I say to you, whatever things you ask when you pray, believe that you receive them, and you will have them.**

Those are great verses, and totally true, but look at the verse that follows right after them: "And whenever you stand praying, if you have anything against anyone, forgive him, that your father in heaven may also forgive you your trespasses" (Mark 11:25). I'm pretty sure the first two verses won't work in our lives unless we obey the last one! And I don't know about you, but I want my father in heaven to forgive my trespasses, don't you? If so, we can see that there's a condition right there. We must forgive.

And just on a side note, I love how Mark 11:25 says, "If you have *anything* against *anyone*." I'm pretty sure that covers your situation and mine, no matter who's to blame! Even people who should know better, even those who don't deserve forgiveness. *Anyone! Anything!* The Bible says there's simply no one we're allowed to hold a grudge against.

I want to show you Mark 11:25 in the Amplified Classic Bible (AMPC), because I think it is such a great illustration of getting free from the ball and chain:

> **And whenever you stand praying, if you have anything against anyone, forgive him and let it drop (leave it, let it go), in order that your Father Who is in heaven may also forgive you your [own] failings and shortcomings and let them drop.**

I love that visual! Just let it drop. Leave it. Let it go. Picture yourself dropping that hurt, that pain (that ball and chain) and just walking away from it, never to return. Leaving it. Letting it go. *That* is a picture of true freedom, my friend. That's how God wants you to live.

Don't Be a Victim

One time I was watching a TV show, and one of the characters, let's call him Dan, ran into an old friend he hadn't seen in years, not since the days when they were Marine pilots together. The two friends went out to dinner to reminisce about old times. But as they sat talking, the friend confided that he and his wife were separated and headed for divorce. Dan felt terrible for his friend and said, "I'm so sorry to hear that. Man, marriage is hard, isn't it?"

In response, the friend spit out sarcastically, "Not for Dan Do-Right." Dan was stunned as his friend followed that barb with a long, bitter diatribe about how perfect Dan's life was, how selfish Dan was, and how it was Dan's fault that he (the friend) had ended up where he was today. When Dan asked him what in the world he was talking about, the friend got increasingly hostile.

"You should have stopped me! It's all your fault!" To Dan's amazement, his friend was talking about an incident 25 years before, when they were serving as Marine pilots. Unbeknownst to Dan, on one fateful night, his friend had an important flight test coming up the next day, but the two of them were out partying into the wee hours, and the friend got roaring drunk.

At 1:00 a.m., he finally told Dan about the next day's flight test, and as soon as Dan heard it, he insisted they should go home. But the friend wanted to keep partying, and they stayed out even later. All of this caused the friend to fail the flight test, which in turn disqualified him from flying in Desert Storm with all his other pilot buddies. Basically, that one decision to stay out late changed the course of his life.

The amazing thing was that he had been bitter toward Dan about it for 25 years. Never mind that it was *his* fault (and not Dan's) that he drank too much and went to bed too late (and never mind that *not* having to fly in Desert Storm was probably a blessing in disguise!). This poor man had harbored this grudge for years and twisted it around in his head until he was the victim of a terrible wrong.

We all know someone like this. When they talk about an issue that hurt them years ago, it sounds as if it happened yesterday. The pain has held them in bondage all that time. That's what unforgiveness can do to you. I wonder if it also caused some of the trouble between him and his wife. I think that's totally possible. Unresolved unforgiveness can have a terrible effect on all the other relationships in our lives too. What a sad story indeed.

Unresolved unforgiveness can have a terrible effect on all the other relationships in our lives too.

Granted, this was a scripted TV drama, not a real situation. But we've probably all heard stories just like this in real life, and the writers may well have drawn from personal experience when they were writing it. It's a fairly common scenario . I know people who have held onto something like that for years.

In one way or another, we've all been done wrong. Forgiveness saves us from becoming a victim. When we forgive, we can leave painful incidents behind and not let them color our future. We can let it go and walk away to live free from torment and a victim mentality.

Hurt by the Church

Another way that Christians can often feel victimized is when they are hurt by someone in church. I think it happens so easily because we expect more from church people. We expect them to behave well, act nice, and be a blessing.

But the reality, of course, is that church is full of *people*, and people have a way of acting however they want to (just like you and me)! Everyone in church is in a different place in their spiritual growth, and no one is perfect.

I have run into a lot of people who are still carrying the wounds of something that happened to them in a church setting, either something the leaders or other church-goers did. Recently I read a wonderful article along these lines, written by one of my former students (a pastor's daughter) and she gave me permission to share it with you:

Have you ever heard the phrase, "I've been hurt by the church?" What does this mean, and why are people "hurt by the church?" Growing up as a pastor's kid and a hard-core church girl, I love the church and I've never really liked that phrase. One reason is that I've seen too many people come and go and do more damage in their own lives by hopping from one church to another (or completely abandoning church or even the Lord) because they've been "hurt by the church." It's more apparent to me now that we need the Lord's help to bring healing and truth to our hearts when it comes to this whole idea of "being hurt by the church."

But, here's why that phrase doesn't sit well with me. YOU are the church. I am the church. WE are the church.

....

YOU are the church. I am the church. WE are the church.

....

The church is not an inanimate object, organization, business, or group; the church is its people. The "church" is not a building or a position — the senior pastors are not "the church," nor are the executive pastors, youth pastors, volunteers, ushers, or small group leaders. You cannot define "the church" as one particular person or staff because the church is made up of all of God's people. Some of these people work at a church, some people work in the marketplace, some of these people work at home ... but regardless, the church IS people (1 Corinthians 12:12–26). These people who make up the church are just that: people! They are all doing their best to follow God and help other people. They are not God; therefore, they are not perfect. Sometimes these people make mistakes in their pursuit to look more like Jesus.

If I were into throwing around the phrase, "I've been hurt by the church," then I would declare myself the chief expert of being "hurt by the church." Why? Because I've grown up in the church and like everyone, I've been hurt by people who say they love Jesus. I've watched my friends, my brothers' friends, my sister's friends, and my parents' friends stop attending our church and, in the process of leaving our church, drag our names through the mud, write blog posts about how they dislike us, tell everyone around them how horrible the church is—the works!

One time, the biggest mentor in my life unfriended me from Facebook when they left the church. I was 17 or 18 at the time and the person who poured into my life the most unfriended me on Facebook. Seems silly, but that's a hard rejection for a 17 or 18-year-old girl to navigate.

As a PK, I've had a front row seat into the beautiful and wonderful, and sometimes bad and ugly, behavior of "the church"—people. Through the years, the Lord has done some intense heart work on me to bring healing to the real hurts. I vividly remember a time when I was 21 and just about to graduate college, laying on the couch in my dorm room crying my eyes out as the Lord had me confront the hurt I felt from people I had trusted, people my parents had poured into and people I had done life with. The Lord walked me through the forgiveness process to release people who had hurt me, my family and our church.

The kicker is that these people were not the least bit sorry about the pain they had caused—yet, I knew I needed to forgive them. So I get it—I get what it's like to be hurt by people who should've known better. I get how it feels to be disappointed by "the church."

On the flip side, I also get what it's like to be the one with thin skin; the one who is too easily offended, or who holds onto a hurt for too long. I've learned that in life, in ministry and in church you have to have thick skin and a tender heart and consistently walk in love and forgiveness.

But here is why I really think "I've been hurt by the church" is a dangerous phrase. This phrase takes away the accountability that we have as Christians to handle our conflict or offense in a mature, responsible and Biblical way. To say, "I've been hurt by the church," means you've been hurt by people. So if you've been "hurt by the church," what you're really saying is that you've been hurt or offended by a person(s).

The Bible tells us what to do when we've been hurt or offended by people and we have a responsibility to handle our offenses God's way. When we use the scapegoat phrase, "I've been hurt by the church," we put a blanket over the real issues we are having with people, so we walk around with a wounded spirit and in the process we drag others into the hurts we have not dealt with.

Instead of being honest, dealing with the hurt in a Biblical way— we just tag it with "the church" and we never have the hard and necessary conversations to resolve the conflict, wounds or hurt we feel. This is not God's will for our lives, so we need his help to deal with the real issue.

I want to encourage you, if you have been "hurt by the church"—I hope you can see there's more to the story. There is an offense or a conflict that God wants to help you resolve. I encourage you to go

before the Lord and ask for his help. I would also recommend look-
ing into some resources on a Biblical way to handle offense. There
are a lot of great books on the topic.

Let's not allow the enemy to divide us —we who are the Church—
through offense, hurt and unresolved conflict. Instead, let's walk
in love and forgiveness and do what Colossians tells us, "Make
allowance for each other's faults, and forgive anyone who offends
you. Remember, the Lord forgave you, so you must forgive others.
Above all, clothe yourselves with love, which binds us all together
in perfect harmony," Colossians 3:13–14.

I pray that God gives us all the grace to be people who are quick to
forgive and slow to get angry and speak poorly of others. That he
helps us make allowances for each other's faults, and the ability to
forgive anyone who offends us. He forgave us, so we can choose to
forgive others. Let's clothe ourselves with his love, which binds us
all together in perfect harmony.

The Root Problem

The longer I'm in ministry, the more I find people with all sorts of
issues. And I've found that these issues may look like one thing, but
the root problem can actually be something else. And very often that
something else is — you guessed it — unforgiveness. Not in every case,
you understand, but often enough to check there first.

Say, for example, you're sick. You've prayed and believed God for
healing, gone to the doctor, taken medication, done everything you
know to try and get better, but nothing works. If that's happening, it's
been my experience that it's good to check your heart for unforgiveness, just to be sure it's not in there clogging your blessing pipe (we'll
talk more about forgiveness and healing in chapter 5).

The same with lack, strife, or other negative activity going on
in your life that isn't part of your covenant in Christ. Simply put,

whenever a bunch of stuff is going wrong in my life, I check my heart for unforgiveness.

Whenever a bunch of stuff is going wrong in my life, I check my heart for unforgiveness.

Many times when I do, the Lord will gently remind me of a small (or big) irritation I let marinate too long that I need to forgive. I've seen it happen over and over in my life and the lives of others.

Tracy's Story: One day I got a phone call from a woman — we'll call her Tracy — who just had so many crazy situations going on in her life. She told me, "Karen, I'm a Bible school graduate and a Bible-believing Christian. I pray, I speak the Word, I know how to rebuke the devil and take my authority. But lately it seems like *everything* in my life is going wrong!"

She proceeded to tell me how her car had broken down, then her dishwasher, and how she'd been demoted at work. Not only that but she found herself still in debt even after getting a consolidation loan, she had gotten sick repeatedly, and several important people in her life were angry or acting out. There was just a lot going on, and none of it good! Life was being so unfair to Tracy.

Don't misunderstand me. Sometimes stuff just happens and life deals us a lot of garbage at once. One minister I know calls that "the stacking theory" where the devil seems to pile on one problem after another, trying to wear us down.

But in this case, I just *happened* to have taught forgiveness in a recent class, so it was fresh in my mind, and it jumped up in my spirit as sometimes happens when I'm counseling people. I was a little hesitant to mention it to Tracy because she sounded like a person who had a vibrant connection with God and wouldn't harbor unforgiveness on purpose. I didn't want to sound accusing, so I sort of soft-peddled it.

"Tracy, just because of a recent subject I've been teaching, can I ask you a question? Is there a chance you're harboring unforgiveness in your heart against anyone? Has anything happened to you lately that caused hurt?" I proceeded to tell her a few stories and verses, just to see if anything rang a bell with her.

After listening for about three minutes, Tracy said, "Oh my gosh, Karen! You're right!" She saw right away that she had been holding onto the hurt from a recent altercation, and it was wreaking havoc in so many other areas of her life. We prayed together to forgive that person, and several weeks later she called back to report that every problem had been resolved.

Wow! Who knew that harboring unforgiveness could be the root of so many other issues? I'm thankful that Tracy was teachable and quick to forgive when God revealed the problem to her.

Maybe you're like Tracy. Maybe an inordinate number of things are going wrong in your life. Or maybe you've been believing for something for a long time and haven't seen results. There could be a number of different reasons, but why not check your heart for unforgiveness to see if it might be clogging your blessing pipe?

Why not check your heart for unforgiveness, to see if it might be clogging your blessing pipe?

It's not hard to do. Just pray, "Father, am I harboring unforgiveness against anyone?" If you are, he'll get the message across to you — he'll tell you who it is. Then make it quick, and forgive them, using the strategies we've talked about so far. You may be surprised by how fast God turns it around for you. He's always ready to help us when we turn to him.

God Will Show the Way

Now let me add a caveat here: don't go looking for trouble. I was once teaching on unforgiveness and a young man came up afterwards, worried that he might have unforgiveness in his heart and not know about it.

Don't worry! If you don't know about it, you're not accountable for it. God loves you. He'll help you and reveal any unforgiveness to you, just like he did for Tracy. He'll show you the way to freedom! I think that unforgiveness is something we need to check our hearts for often, but don't go looking for trouble. If he nudges you, maybe through a sermon or a comment from a friend or a phone call (like Tracy's with me) or even as you're reading this book, and tells you "you need to forgive so-and-so" just do it!

It's okay to ask him as often as you want, "Lord, is there anyone I need to forgive?" Especially if anything weird is going on in your life, if suddenly your business dries up, or healing doesn't come, or everything starts breaking down, or you have unusual money troubles, etc. I remember talking to one man who's business was suffering and the Lord prompted him to forgive someone. Within a week, several customers who had been slow in paying sent him all the money they owed, *plus* a long-pending lawsuit was settled in his favor. God will always show us the way to forgiveness!

Questions for Reflection and Discussion >>

• What caused you to pick up this book?

• How have you been hurt?

• How do you fill in the blank, "I forgive you, but _____
_____."

• Which stories, if any, resonated with you?

• Which scriptures helped you the most?

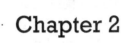

Chapter 2

When People Hurt You

Sheila's Story: Once I was ministering at a women's retreat in the beautiful mountains of Eastern Oregon. There were only about 30 of us, so we just held the ministry meetings in the living room of one of the condos where we were staying. It was a cozy environment, and God met us there in a powerful way.

For two solid days I ministered to the women about forgiveness. We had meetings morning, noon and night, so they heard at least eight hours' worth of God's Word on the subject, how he had forgiven us, how we can forgive others, and the freedom that it can bring to our lives.

The women were scattered around the living room on various couches and chairs as they listened, but in the very back of the room, there was one woman — let's call her Sheila — who sat through all the meetings on the hearth of the fireplace. Because she was behind everyone else, I was the only one who could see her face, and I noticed that through every meeting, she was crying. Not big boo-hoo type crying:

she just had tears silently streaming down her face the whole time, and she occasionally wiped them away with a tissue.

I remember thinking, "Gosh, I hope she doesn't get dehydrated!" (I actually found myself offering her bottled water during our fellowship and meal times!) It was obvious that the messages hit home with Sheila in a powerful way, and I prayed that God was doing a work in her heart.

At the end of the last evening meeting, I had all the women write in their Bibles the name of the person(s) they needed to forgive and date it, and then I led them in a prayer of forgiveness. After that, we all went to bed.

The next morning before we headed back to civilization, we had one final meeting and the women shared testimonies about how the teaching had impacted their lives. I was thrilled by all that God had done. And at the very end, Sheila raised her hand, and I couldn't wait to hear what she had to say.

"I Just Couldn't Forgive"

She started out by saying, "Last night, I slept through the night for the first time in 20 years."

Her announcement was greeted with stunned silence. I wondered if everyone was thinking the same thing I was thinking: "She hasn't slept through the night in 20 years? How horrible!" (Apparently, unforgiveness can keep you awake at night.)

Sheila went on to tell us that when she was a child, her family joined a cult where members sell all their worldly goods and go to live together on a ranch. I don't know how long they lived there, but from Sheila's point of view, it was a terrible time, and in the end her parents got divorced and their whole family was thrown into chaos.

You can imagine how that affected Sheila's life. In her child-mind, this cult had torn her family apart. She especially hated the cult leader who was at the very core of destroying all that she loved.

As she grew older, no matter how hard she tried, she couldn't shake the despair and pain of her childhood (as evidenced by her sleepless nights). Many times fellow Christians would tell her, "You need to forgive that cult leader and put this behind you."

Sheila knew they were right, but she just couldn't let it go. As she told this part of the story, she began crying again and said with teeth clenched, "I tried over and over to forgive him, but the pain went too deep, and *I just couldn't*. I still just hated what he had done to my family." To add to her pain, the cult leader had died, so now there would never be retribution or vindication because he would never apologize or get what she felt he deserved.

Isn't that horrible? My heart went out to her. I couldn't imagine begin trapped in this cycle of unforgiveness, being angry at a dead man. What a hopeless feeling.

Thankfully, her story didn't end there. After hearing God's Word on forgiveness for all those hours at this retreat, she began to realize she *could* forgive that cult leader. And of course, his was the name that Sheila wrote in her Bible the night before. She said the moment she prayed to forgive him; she felt a weight lift off her. She said it was the most peaceful, wonderful feeling! And that night, she slept like a log for the first time in years.

"I Forgive You, But I Still Hate You!"

At that retreat, I realized that it's one thing to know that we *should* forgive, but it's a whole other thing to be able to do it. Many have tried and failed, just like Sheila.

But look what happened when she was able to soak her spirit in God's Word until she knew that forgiveness was not only possible, but that she could do it. She received the faith for it because faith — even the faith for forgiveness — comes by hearing and hearing by the Word of God (Rom. 10:17).

Sometimes in your life the hurt goes so deep, and it's been there so long, you have to have supernatural help to be set free. But you *do* have supernatural help. When the Word of God is dwelling in you richly (Col. 3:16), you can overcome!

Obviously, if you are still harboring hatred in your heart towards anyone, you haven't forgiven them, just like Sheila hadn't. True forgiveness is to release the one who has done you wrong. God wants your heart to be free from hatred, and forgiveness is the way to get there. One thing you have to understand is that forgiveness is a faith proposition, not a feeling!

Forgiveness is a faith proposition, not a feeling!

I heard someone once say it this way: forgiveness is the decision you make *once*, forgetting is the decision you make *daily*. I think that says it perfectly! It helps me know that I shouldn't be surprised when *feelings* resurface after I've forgiven someone.

Don't Let Feelings Fool You

Feelings follow *after* faith. Many of us can say that we've *tried* to forgive, but like Sheila, we found the horrible feelings come back to choke us. But here's what I want you to know — feelings have nothing to do with faith.

That's why this book has three steps. First we look at stories and principles of forgiveness, then we meditate on God's Word about it, then we write down who we forgave and when. That way, when the thoughts and feelings come crashing back (and trust me, they probably will!) and we're tempted to think, "oh no, I didn't forgive!" we can each point to what we've written and say, "Too late, devil – I already forgave them. It's done. Now my feelings have to line up with what the Bible says."

Then we can go back to step 2 to review and speak the Word for a while, until our mind is renewed and our spirit can dominate our flesh. I want you to know that's a normal process for anyone who chooses to forgive. Don't let the feelings fool you. Sometimes it takes a while to renew your mind to forgiveness, and your feelings often have to catch up.

Don't let the feelings fool you.

Romans 12:2 says, "Do not be conformed to this world, but be transformed by the renewing of your mind." I like the way the Living Bible says it: "Don't copy the behavior and customs of this world, but be a new and different person with a fresh newness in all you do and think. Then you will learn from your own experience how his ways will really satisfy you." That says it all, don't you think? Don't copy the behaviors of this world!

One thing the world tells us is to hold a grudge — make someone pay for what they've done to you. Don't let someone get away with it. Get revenge! But we can see that the Bible says don't conform to that way of thinking — don't copy it. Instead, be a new and different person with a fresh newness in all you do and think. Be transformed.

One of the definitions in Merriam-Webster's dictionary for the word *transformed* is "To change in character or condition." Renewing our mind to think the way God does about forgiveness supernaturally changes the condition of a hurting heart.

Renewing our mind is really just changing our thoughts to agree with God's thoughts. In Isaiah 55:9, God says, "For as the heavens are higher than the earth, so are My ways higher than your ways, and My thoughts than your thoughts."

God's not saying to us, "Ha ha, my thoughts are higher than yours!" He's saying, "Come on up and think like I think — this is where the freedom is!" We do that by reading his Word. His Word is his will for your life. It's his thoughts. When we study and meditate his thoughts, we replace wrong, worldly thinking with his higher thinking that leads to peace and freedom.

When we think like God thinks, we can live like he lives. He's never worried, never sick, never lacking, never wondering how things will turn out. I want to live like that! So first, I need to think like that. So I read his word to *change* (renew) my thinking into his thinking.

How To Change Your Thoughts

When it comes to forgiving, very often the tricky part is shutting down the crazy self-talk that rehearses an incident over and over in your mind.

If you just keep thinking on what happened (or how you felt, or what they said, or the results of all that), you aren't going to be able to walk in forgiveness and have the peace God has promised. And when you don't forgive, by default you give that hurtful person (or people or event) permission to stay in your mind and continually cause pain.

"When you don't forgive, by default you give that hurtful person permission to stay in your mind and continually cause pain."

So how can you stop thinking about it and take dominion over your thoughts? Well, you could try closing your eyes tight and saying, "I won't think about this. I won't think about this. I won't think about this!"

Have you ever tried that? I have! And you know what happens? In eight seconds or less it's back in your mind again, right? Trying not to think about it just doesn't work.

So instead of trying to "will" yourself to stop thinking about something, we have to *replace* those thoughts. We have to put something *else* in our mind. And the best thing to put in there is God's Word. The Bible is truth, and truth is what makes us free (see John 17:17; John 8:32).

That's the step 2 part of this book, filling our heart and mind with what God says, and declaring that word with our own mouth until it becomes a reality in our lives. I like to call it "thought replacement therapy." When we flood our minds with what God says (his Word), we flush out the wrong kind of thinking that holds us in pain and bondage.

Think of it like this: Picture a glass full of dark liquid that represents wrong thoughts, and you want to empty the glass (like you want to empty your mind of painful thoughts). How would you do it? The obvious answer is to tip the glass and pour out the liquid, right? But since we can't tip you over to empty your brain, let's rule that out.

So how can you get rid of the dark liquid? You *displace* it. Start with a big bucket full of pure, clear, spring water which, in our analogy here, represents right thoughts in line with the Word of God. When you start pouring the water into the glass full of dark liquid, and you keep pouring and pouring and pouring, what will eventually happen? The clean water will *displace* the dark liquid and soon enough, you'd have a glass full of nothing but beautiful, crystal-clear water. All signs of the dark liquid would be gone.

It's the same with those painful, crazy-cycle thoughts. The best way to change them is to *replace* them with good thoughts. And the Word of God is the perfect replacement. When you pour the cleansing water of the Word into your mind by thinking on what God has said, your mind is filled with beautiful crystal-clear thoughts of peace, love, grace and forgiveness.

Simply put, in order to get *wrong thoughts out*, you need to put *right thoughts in*. It takes effort, but you can do it! Use step 2 to help you.

....

In order to get wrong thoughts out, you need to put right thoughts in.

....

But be warned, your mind *will* try to wander back to that painful person or event. That's when you need to double your dose of the Word. Keep *choosing* to think on what God has said. Second Corinthians 10:5 says it this way: "Casting down arguments and every high thing that exalts itself against the knowledge of God, bringing every thought into captivity to the obedience of Christ."

Every thought! That takes some effort. That's why it's written down for you in step 2, so in those times when your mind starts rehearsing the pain again, you can grab this book and start saying what God says! You'll be surprised by how quickly and effectively that works to get your mind back on the right things because there is power in your words. Mark 11:23 says you can have whatever you say, and Romans 4:17 tells you to call those things that be not as though they are. Just as God created the world with words, he's given you the same power. When you speak God's Word, you're agreeing with it in faith, and releasing God's power into your life!

You Are the CEO of Your Thoughts

Remember, you (and only you) are in charge of what you think about. I like to say it this way: you are the CEO of your thoughts. You are not a victim; you have the power! So use it to your advantage. When wrong thoughts come say, "No, I take those thoughts captive. I remember what God's promises say."

Again, that's why I've written the promises and declarations down for you in step 2. It's very much like a bank account. You can't withdraw money from your account unless you've first made a deposit. You have to put God's Word *in* (read it, declare it, spend time with it) so that it's in your mind and in your mouth when you need it.

If you spend all your time in the crazy-cycle, thinking about the person who has hurt you or the bad thing that has happened, you're going to get stuck. The only way to forgive and leave the pain behind is to change what you're thinking on.

The only way to forgive and leave the pain behind is to change what you're thinking on.

One minister friend of mine says it this way: "It's a beautiful gift to be able to direct our own thoughts. We can either choose to set up camp in miserable circumstances of defeat, or we can push each thought through the filter of who God is. What you're going through may be really hard, but he hasn't left you once. He is faithful. He speaks words of life and hope over you. He is the One who restores your soul. So train your thoughts to think on him, to point to his goodness. You are *not* a victim of your circumstance. Know him, think on him, speak of him."

When we take control of our thoughts, we are in the power position. Isaiah 26:3 says, "You will keep him in perfect peace, whose mind is stayed on You, because he trusts in You." Put yourself in that verse: God will keep you in perfect peace when your mind (thoughts) are fixed on him because you trust in him. What a wonderful promise! When you keep your thoughts in line with God's, trusting everything he has told you and everything He's doing in your life, you can have perfect peace.

What If They Did It on Purpose?

Sometimes people hurt us and they didn't mean to. It still hurts, and we still need to forgive them, of course. But the rubber really meets the road when someone hurts us *on purpose*. Gah! Is God asking us to forgive someone who is just plain mean and calculating against us, someone who has gone out of their way to do us wrong?

Well, you might not like it, but the answer is yes. Because God doesn't *ever* want you to suffer any of the pain that comes from unforgiveness! In Matthew 5:44 Jesus says, "But I say to you, love your enemies, bless those who curse you, do good to those who hate you, and pray for those who *spitefully* use you and persecute you."

Yeowza. Talk about changing your thoughts to match God's thoughts; that verse has *all* opposite thoughts than our natural human thinking, doesn't it? But Jesus is trying to help us here. And he's telling us that even if someone *spitefully* uses us and persecutes us (on purpose!), we're to love and pray for them. I'm pretty sure that includes forgiving them.

Is Jesus asking the impossible of us? Of course not. If it's in the Bible, we can do it! He's showing us the path to freedom and peace.

When we choose forgiveness, we choose to obey him, and that undermines everything the devil is trying to do in our lives through someone else. Forgiveness is choosing the high road, so to speak, and kicking the whole situation into supernatural overdrive. We don't want to muck around in the lowland of retaliation, revenge, and grudge-holding. There's no victory there.

Forgiveness is choosing the high road and kicking the whole situation into supernatural overdrive.

Plus, when you choose to forgive — even someone who did you wrong on purpose — you're keeping your blessing pipe clear! Forgiveness takes away all the sting. It puts the matter into God's hands and guarantees you'll come out on top.

When They Aren't Sorry

Gina's Story: I was chatting with a woman at my gym — let's call her Gina — just as we finished our workout. Although we didn't know each other well, we had met a couple of times before and Gina knew that I wrote books. She asked me if I was writing a book at the time, and when I told her yes, she asked what it was about. When I told her it was about forgiveness, she got a knowing look.

"Oh wow, forgiveness" she said, "that's such a hard thing!"

I asked what she meant, and she proceeded to tell me her story. Several years ago, just before her mother had died, Gina's sister (who is a Christian and works at a church) went to their mother's bank, apparently told a series of lies, and somehow managed to withdraw $90,000 of their mother's money. She then gave the money to the church where she worked. Gina explained to me that the money was meant to be the mother's inheritance to *all four* of her children, which included Gina and her other two siblings. Gina's mother passed away soon after that, and that's when all the siblings found out that their sister had already taken most of the money and given it to the church.

Gina was *so* hurt by what her sister had done. I could tell it wasn't just that she didn't get her inheritance, but she felt so betrayed by her sister. The fact that her sister was a Christian just added salt to the wound. Like many of us she expected someone in ministry, who claimed to be a follower of God, to act better. Gina expected more from someone religious and from the church.

The whole episode caused Gina and her family a lot of grief, and they remained estranged from their sister. Besides that, it left a bad taste in Gina's mouth concerning the church. She told me, "It was so against what I expected from a Christian and a church — they were basically stealing our money!"

Later, Gina went so far as to meet her sister with a mediator in an attempt to gain some understanding between the two, and possibly see about recovering some of the money. But the meeting didn't produce the results Gina had hoped for. The two sisters didn't come to any kind of understanding. Even worse, her sister had made up a story in her head that justified her actions. She never acknowledged any wrongdoing (and wasn't at all repentant) because she had twisted it around in her own mind. She didn't think she'd done anything wrong in taking all of her mother's money. This was amazing to Gina.

When someone does us wrong they should be sorry, not justify themselves or refuse to admit it.

You can imagine how that just added to Gina's hurt and anger. When someone does us wrong they should be sorry, not justify themselves or refuse to admit it. That's just so unfair and makes us so mad!

"He Just Laughs at Me"

Yolanda's Story: I knew another young woman in my church years ago — let's call her Yolanda — whose story, while not exactly the same, parallels Gina's in terms of someone hurting her and being unrepentant about it.

I was teaching a series of sermons on forgiveness on Sunday mornings, and after the second message, Yolanda made an appointment with me. As she sat across the desk from me in my office, I could tell she was very agitated.

"Pastor Karen, I understand what you've been saying about forgiveness these past Sunday mornings," she said, "and I know it's important to forgive. But I'm struggling with it." It turned out that Yolanda's father had sexually abused her as a child, but when she confronted him about it years later, he would never admit he'd done anything wrong.

"He still just laughs at me, saying he never did that," she told me with tears. "I've tried to forgive him, but all I can see in my mind is his face, laughing at me. He's not sorry at all for what he's done to me!"

I felt so bad for her. How frustrating to confront someone who has injured you beyond words, and have them laugh at you. Part of me wanted to join her in a plan to punch his lights out. But I knew that wasn't the answer for her. Revenge feels good to the flesh (for an hour or maybe even for a week), but forgiveness is the only way to be truly free.

Revenge feels good to the flesh, but forgiveness is the only way to be truly free.

Yolanda and I spent a few sessions together, going over what the Bible said about forgiveness, and like many before her, the Word did a work on her heart and mind and she was able to completely forgive him.

And amazingly enough, once she did that, so many other things in her life starting falling into order. She began to have wonderful friendships, not realizing that unforgiveness had caused her to hold people at arm's length. Among other things, she also received a raise at her job, and was able to get control of her financial life. It's amazing what begins to happen when a person is able to forgive and "unclog their blessing pipe."

"I Forgive You, But I Want You To Be Sorry!"

Maybe you can identify with Gina's or Yolanda's stories. Maybe someone has hurt you and they justify it in their own mind or to others. Maybe they even deny that it happened. Maybe they're just not sorry at all.

When someone hurts or betrays us, our natural reaction is that we want them to be really, really sorry. Right? We want them to feel bad and regret their behavior and own up to everything. We want them to know how badly they've hurt us, to acknowledge their wrongdoing — at the very *least* to say they're sorry, and if life went the way it should, they should even make it right!

But of course it doesn't always happen that way, as we can see from these two stories.

Here's what I want you to get: the person who has hurt you may never say they're sorry. Never! They may even tell everyone that *you* are the problem. They may never take responsibility for what they've done. They may never reach out to you or attempt to make peace.

And while that might make you really mad, it's important that you come to grips with it. If you're waiting for an apology or admittance of wrongdoing, it might never come, and then where will you be?

The person who has hurt you may never say they're sorry.

You'll be still stuck in unforgiveness with all its horrible side-effects working in your life. Waiting for an apology from someone who hurt you is giving them way too much power over your life.

Because really, them being sorry (or not) has nothing to do with forgiveness. Remember, we don't forgive people because they deserve it. We forgive because God has told us to in his Word. We do it to obey him and because that's the way to freedom for us, whether they admit wrongdoing or not.

We forgive because Jesus is our example. When he was hanging on the cross, completely innocent, betrayed by his disciples, bruised and beaten beyond recognition to pay the price for *our* sin, he said, "Father forgive them, for they know not what they do" (Luke 23:34). None of us have suffered as he did, yet he forgave. We can too.

So let this truth set you free: forgiveness isn't about the person who hurt you, it's about you obeying God and keeping your heart right. It's about cutting the chain and walking away from the pain of the past, keeping your blessing pipe clear.

What Forgiveness Is *Not*

We humans think differently about forgiveness than God does. But freedom lies in renewing your mind to what God thinks about it, as we've said. One good place to start thinking differently about forgiveness is to talk about what it's *not*. For one thing, forgiveness is not condoning what someone has done.

Merriam-Webster's dictionary defines *condoning* as "brushing off, excusing, discounting, disregarding, glossing over, or overlooking." I think sometimes we feel like if we forgive, we're saying what happened is okay with us, that we're just brushing it off or glossing over what someone did. Part of us thinks "I have to hold onto this so that everyone knows an injustice was done here!"

Forgiveness does not mean that we're pretending something never happened, and we're not excusing what they did. We're not saying it's okay with us. Forgiveness is not validating someone's actions; it's freeing us from their actions. When we choose to forgive, we're simply obeying God and getting free.

I think we humans tend to think that forgiving someone shows weakness, like we're rolling over and letting someone treat us in whatever abusive way they want to. Far from it! Forgiving someone does *not* mean being a doormat.

....

Forgiving someone does not mean being a doormat.

....

Hugo's Story: When I was a Bible school instructor, I used to teach the subject of forgiveness every year in a class called Blood Covenant.

One day after I taught it, an older student — let's call him Hugo — came to my office after class. Hugo was a businessman from another country, and he had left his business in the care of his business partner while he came to school in America. Unfortunately he discovered, over time, that his business partner had stolen from him and from the employees, and Hugo was forced to sue him. Hugo asked me, "Karen, you say I must forgive this man who stole from me and my employees. Does that mean I just let him get away with it? Am I not allowed to take him to court?"

I assured Hugo that that's not what forgiveness means. Forgiveness is a heart issue. First we are to take care of that issue in our hearts by forgiving. Then yes, we might have to take some action in the natural.

If an employee, for example, is stealing from the company or treating another employee badly, of course he must be reprimanded, or perhaps even penalized, fired or sued. If a child is being bullied in school, of course action must be taken. If someone has been abusive or even killed someone, they must face the consequences and be held accountable for their actions. And the same is true in many other situations, including heated disagreements of any kind.

Many times a situation will call for a confrontation. Forgiveness is not ignoring or walking away from someone when a conflict needs to be resolved. In fact, being angry at someone without telling them about it isn't really fair. If there is disagreement, be willing to talk things through.

In other words, there is a practical, natural side to this. If someone has stolen from you or committed a crime of any kind, it's okay to take legal action against them. If there are issues happening in everyday life that need to be confronted, then do it. Just forgive first. It's just not okay to harbor unforgiveness against them while you're doing it. For your own heart's sake.

"I Forgive You, But I Don't Want You to Get Away with It!"

Understandably, Hugo didn't want his business partner getting away with stealing. Suing him was the right thing to do, as long as Hugo forgave him first.

I think many times we hold a grudge against someone because if we don't, we think they might "get away with it." From the spiritual side, you can trust God on this one. Galatians 6:7 says, "Do not be deceived, God is not mocked; for whatever a man sows, that he will also reap." God is not mocked means he is no fool! He knows all about human nature; he's seen it all, and he says that whatever a person sows, that will he also reap.

In other words, you don't have to worry about someone getting away with what they've done. God's got it covered. You do what you have to in the natural, but in your heart you can forgive, leaving "payback" to him. When you forgive, you're turning the person and the situation over to God and letting him work (we'll talk more about that in chapter 3, Setting the Captive Free).

There is also the element of wanting someone to truly understand that what they've done is wrong. In other words, we want them to learn from their mistake, or at least keep them from doing it to someone else. But in the end, we can't make someone repent for their behavior. Our part is to forgive and turn them over to God.

Very often, we want payback when someone has hurt us. The concept of *revenge* is very familiar to us in today's world. It's the theme for endless movies and books and even wars and global skirmishes. The idea of "don't get mad, just get even" is very prevalent in this day and age.

....
Very often, we want payback when someone has hurt us.
....

But God doesn't want you or me to have to deal with revenge. Romans 12:19 says, "Never take your own revenge, beloved, but leave room for the wrath of God, for it is written, "Vengeance is Mine, I will repay," says the Lord" (NASB). God is telling us not to take revenge upon ourselves. Leave room for his wrath. Let him take care of it. He knows how to repay.

I once heard Oral Roberts talk about this verse and he said: "Do you know why God said vengeance — or revenge — is his, not ours? Because revenge is too hard on the human heart." That's God, always watching out for our hearts. Proverbs 4:23 says, "Above all else, guard your heart, for everything you do flows from it." Forgiveness is one way we guard our hearts.

The Issue of Trust

Now there's a big difference between holding someone accountable and holding a grudge. Accountability is necessary; holding a grudge (harboring unforgiveness) is harmful. *You* know if you've forgiven someone or not. Yes, you might have to sue someone like Hugo did, but do it *after* you've prayed and forgiven them. If, as you're taking them to court, the vein stands out in your neck and you're spitting mad as you say between gritted teeth, "I'm going to get even," then you know you haven't forgiven them yet.

Forgiveness is a heart issue. Take care of the heart issue *inside* first, then proceed with the natural issues that need to be handled *outside*. Be sure you have forgiven before you take any necessary natural action against them (and be sure it's necessary. Ask God!).

When you've forgiven someone for hurting you, it doesn't mean you have to trust them ever again. You don't have to be best friends with them or even be around them (unless that's something beyond your control).

I heard someone say it like this: forgiveness is what we're commanded to do, but trust must be earned. If a situation warrants it — if you're in danger physically, emotionally, or any other way — it's important to set appropriate boundaries with someone who has done you wrong. It's okay to forgive and stay away.

It's okay to forgive and stay away.

If it's possible, repair the broken trust. Romans 12:18 says, "If it is possible, as much as depends on you, live peaceably with all men." But notice that says *if* it's possible — sometimes it's not — and as much as it depends on *you*. You can only control what depends on you. You can't force someone else to repent, change, or live peaceably with you.

Sometimes you've done all you can to restore relationship and trust, but the other party isn't willing or acting appropriately. Then you have to set the boundaries in a way that will protect you and those you are responsible for. Sometimes it's just best for everyone if you separate yourself from them. As one friend of mine says, "It's easier for me to forgive a really difficult person and walk in love with them if I don't have to see them."

One lady told me, "I thought forgiving meant I was also supposed to allow that person to have full access again — to get all their privileges of relationship back. Once I learned it was okay to separate the two, I was able to forgive. Restoration and trust [are] possible, but only if behaviors change. Forgiveness is truly for us and can happen even if the other person never says sorry or changes."

My friend, forgiveness doesn't mean you have to continue a relationship with someone who's hurt you. Romans 16:17 even tells us, "I urge you, brethren, note those who cause divisions and offenses . . . and avoid them." Just because you have forgiven someone — or have to continually forgive them — doesn't mean you have to trust them again.

Seek the Lord and ask him if it's better for you to separate yourself. In other words, you don't have to keep putting yourself in position to be hurt or taken advantage of. All you have to do is forgive them so that your heart is free.

Forgiveness Does *Not* Always Require a Face-to-Face

Here's another question people often ask me: "Do I have to tell the person face-to-face that I've forgiven them?" My answer is "Sometimes." (How's that for a definite course of action?)

The thing is, every situation is different. Only the Lord knows what's required of you in a certain situation — what's required to set you completely free. He knows everything that's going on and *both* sides of the story, so *ask him.* "Lord, do I need to go and talk to them? Go in person to tell them I've forgiven them or even apologize? Do we need to communicate and work it through?"

Sometimes he will impress upon your heart that it's necessary to do that. If he is prompting you in that direction, don't fight it. If you'll step out in faith and obedience, and be willing to talk with the person face-to-face, he will be there to help you. And when you obey that nudge, you'll end up free. It can turn out better than you even expect.

The Bible even gives us instruction how to approach someone who has done us wrong. (Don't you love how applicable the Bible is? It's our instruction manual for life!) Matthew 18:15–17 says:

> **Moreover if your brother sins against you, go and tell him his fault between you and him alone. If he hears you, you have gained your brother. [16] But if he will not hear, take with you one or two more, that "by the mouth of two or three witnesses every word may be established." And if he refuses to hear them, tell it to the church. [17] But if he refuses even to hear the church, let him be to you like a heathen and a tax collector.**

After you've prayed and forgiven someone, and if the Lord instructs you to approach them (to either apologize or let them know there's no unforgiveness between you), notice there are several steps to this face-to-face deal.

First the Bible says to go and tell him (or her) "between you and him alone." For the most part, we humans don't do this. If someone does us wrong, our first inclination is to go tell someone else — and maybe a lot of someone else's — because we want people to take our side and understand from our point of view just how we've been wronged. We want to assemble a team that's "on our side."

We want people to take our side and understand from our point of view just how we've been wronged.

Sadly, that's completely unscriptural. So of course it won't turn out well. It's not going to help rectify the situation, and it's not going to in any way set you free. The only reason you should ever tell anyone else is to do what verse 16 says: to take someone along when you confront the issues. (You only do this, though, if they didn't listen to you when you went the first time, "between you and him alone.")

Now when it comes to taking someone else along, it doesn't mean to take someone who's "on your side." It means take someone who is mature, godly, able to see both sides, and who may act as a mediator or peacemaker between the two of you.

This is good thing to do if the situation is volatile, and I'm sure it's why the Bible tells us to do it. If you've tried to approach someone before (as this scripture instructs us to do) and they wouldn't listen, you need someone else along. Just by being there, a third-party can help everyone remain calm, and can also provide an unbiased viewpoint of what actually happened. Otherwise it's just your word against the other person's.

The third step, if these first two don't work, is to go to a higher authority, but only after you've tried the first two! Many people like to skip steps one and two and just call in the big guns. Kind of like six-year-olds: "Mom! He took my_____!" Some of us turn into six-year-olds when we've been hurt or we're in strife with someone. We want the authority figure to step in and fix everything for us. But that's another subject for another day.

Let me say this as a sidenote:, if you're a parent, it's a great idea to teach these biblical strategies to your children, and help them learn early how to diffuse situations of strife and work out disagreements among themselves without having to tattle to mom or dad. Think of how peaceful your life would be!

Back to the higher authority. In this instance, the Bible says it's the church, but it can also apply to the boss, the governing organization, the parent, etc. Notice it's only if all three of those strategies don't work that you're allowed to stop talking with this person or eliminate them from your life.

All that being said, sometimes you don't have to have any contact at all in order to forgive. While confronting is sometimes very necessary to the process, sometimes it's not. This is where you pray and ask God what you need to do.

Sometimes there's no person to approach. Sometimes you don't even know them. Sometimes they're dead! Sometimes you're forgiving an entity rather one specific person. And sometimes you're forgiving yourself (see more about that in chapter 7).

You get the idea. The only way to know if you have to face the person you've harbored a grudge against is to ask God. He will always steer you right. His only goal is your freedom. Sometimes that means restored relationships too. Always listen closely to what he instructs you to do, and obey him quickly.

Forgiving Again (and Again)

In Matthew 18:21, Peter asks Jesus a question about forgiveness that we have all probably asked: "Lord, how often shall my brother sin against me, and I forgive him? Up to seven times?" Peter is using all his faith here. He is feeling like a spiritual giant, being willing to forgive someone *up to seven times*!

I'm sure he expected Jesus to say something like, "Wow, Peter, you are awesome. You're willing to forgive somebody seven times? That is so mature!"

But what does Jesus say? "I do not say to you, up to seven times, but up to seventy times seven" (v. 22). Yikes! *How* many times do I have to forgive someone, Jesus? If we do the math there, Jesus is telling Peter to forgive someone 490 times. *Per day.* That's a lot of times, probably more times than most of us have ever been called upon to forgive someone.

But here's the deal: I don't even think that Jesus was telling Peter that he had to forgive someone 490 times a day, do you? I don't think Jesus meant that on the four hundredth and ninety-first time someone did him wrong (should he ever get that far), it would be okay to stop forgiving and hold a grudge. No! What Jesus is really telling Peter (and us) is that we must forgive every time. He *never* wants us to be in bondage to unforgiveness.

We must forgive every time. Jesus never wants us to be in bondage to unforgiveness.

So that means there are times we might just have to forgive someone *multiple* times, even in the same day. We might live with this person, or work with them, or have them as a permanent fixture in our lives.

I don't know about you, but it's not great news to me that I might have to forgive someone again and again. But when I'm faced with a situation like that, I remind myself that if the Bible says to do it, I can do it! I'm not doing it in my own strength, I'm leaning on God to help me.

Ephesians 6:10 says to "be strong in the Lord and in the power of *his* might" — not mine. He is standing by, ready to help me when I cry out, "Father, help me forgive them again!"

When You Have To See Them Often

I have one friend who was abused by family members as she was growing up, which meant she had to see them on a regular basis, even after she became a Christian and forgave them.

Gail's Story: "I found it extremely hard to forgive family members that had taken advantage of me sexually. At first, seeing them at family functions made the hate I felt towards them grow deeper. I resented having to smile as if they'd done nothing wrong."

Gail shared with me that it's been a process she's had to work through, and it's not always been easy. "Sometimes when I see a family member that used me in my past, I have to continue to actively forgive," she says, "especially if they say something that brings up anger."

But Gail has stayed faithful to meditating God's Word and diligently asking for his help, and she reports that even with little flare-ups, she's no longer in bondage to the pain.

"Forgiveness is 100% worth it!" she says. "There is a freedom and a peace that I received when I forgave. For me, forgiveness is not an option. I love peace and freedom, so forgiving is an absolute must!"

Now, remember what we just said about boundaries and trust. You don't have to continually put yourself in a position to be wronged or harmed. Go back and read that again if you need to! But when we tend to matters of the heart and do things God's way by forgiving, He is working in our situation. We can expect a supernatural outcome and we can expect peace and freedom in our heart (which is the only heart we can really be in charge of).

Sheri's Story: While I was writing this book, I heard from a former student of mine — let's call her Sheri — who had been listening to a CD of my class on forgiveness, and she learned something great. Here's what she said: "I tend to forgive and let stuff go really easily. But there's been a certain situation in which a person who I see continually is often saying and doing hurtful things to me.

"I know she's just struggling with something internally and it's not intentional because, as you taught us, hurting people hurt people. She doesn't see what she's doing. I thought I was making a conscious effort to forgive, but in your teaching, you said "it's not okay to stay hurt." That was an ah-ha moment for me! I realized I was still holding on to feeling hurt. I had never put together that feeling hurt equates to unforgiveness.

"So I forgave right there in my car, driving down the interstate. As a result, I started sleeping again at night, which hasn't happened in the months this has been going on. It was so freeing! I'm still in the same situation that I've been in, nothing has changed with this lady, she's still treating me the same. But I am different! I am free! I'm at such a place of peace and am able to show God's love to her instead of feeling hurt all the time.

"I'm also believing that my choice to walk in love with this lady will leave room for God to work in her heart. I'm excited to see what God is going to do!"

God *never* wants you in bondage to unforgiveness, no matter what has happened. You *never* want to let your heart be poisoned by harboring a grudge, and you never want to clog your blessing pipe. So no matter how many times you have to forgive in a day or how often you have to see the other person, forgiveness is always the right thing to do. It always brings God into the situation, and it always brings freedom in your life.

Forgiving After Divorce

I know many people who have gone through the pain of divorce. And you've probably heard the saying, "God hates divorce" — which is true — but he hates it because it has such a devastating effect on the hearts of the couple and the hearts of those around them. Get that straight in your mind. He hates divorce, but he doesn't hate *you* or anyone else in the situation, which means there can be forgiveness and restoration after divorce.

There are as many varied reasons and dynamics for divorce as there are people. But in order to move forward after a divorce, you must forgive everyone involved, including yourself (we'll get to forgiving yourself in chapter 7).

In order to move forward after a divorce, you must forgive everyone involved, including yourself.

As many people would testify, forgiving an ex can be complicated. This is especially true if there are children involved, because then as parents you have to stay involved with each other. Maintaining a civil relationship most likely requires forgiving again and again.

Megan's Story: While some couples (and families) remain civil through a divorce, I have a friend — let's call her Megan — whose divorce was anything but civil. Her ex was abusive and mean and so was his family, and they all pitted the three children against Megan. Without going into a lot of detail, the list of horrors went on and on.

It's been a few years now, and I wanted to include Megan's story here. Although no one emerges unscathed from such an experience, today Megan has carved out a new life for herself and is happy and thriving. I knew forgiveness was a big part of that, so I asked her to share a bit of her journey. Here's what she said:

"Yes, I've forgiven my ex-husband, and yes, it's been over and over! With divorce, if you have kids, you can't separate yourself from your ex completely. You can set boundaries, but you'll always have them in your life.

"For me, it's been a journey, and it is hard! I'd ask the Holy Spirit to help me forgive him, and then he would do something mean and I was right back where I started, so angry at him. But I knew Jesus said to bless your enemies (Matt. 5:44), and even on the cross, Jesus cried to the Father to forgive those who tortured and killed him (Luke 23:34).

"So, I started with simply saying, 'God, I forgive him. Bless him Father.' That was all I said, over and over and over, every day. Then, I gave myself a measuring stick. If every action he took against me resulted in me becoming angry and depressed, then I needed to look at my heart. If any wrong brought me back to wanting him to die (and die painfully!), then I knew I wasn't in forgiveness.

"It took me a couple years to get to a place where I could look at him and just feel compassion for him. I could see the things that happened in his life that he had no control over, such as growing up in an abusive home. I could realize that hurting people hurt people, which had led to the abuse in our home.

"I knew his own choices had affected him and I felt sorry for him. That enabled me to realize that he needed God just as much as I did, so I started praying for him. I still have to remind myself of that. I still have to examine my heart, and know it's not my job to examine his.

"Also — I'm being completely honest here — I had to deal with the fact that he didn't seem to suffer any consequences for his actions. He has remarried and has a big house and a position at a church. But I've had to accept the fact that's between him and God, not me.

"And things aren't perfect in his life, either, of course. When I found out about some things that aren't going great for him, instead of rejoicing, I felt compassion for him. That's when I realized that forgiveness really had taken place in me. That doesn't mean we don't have issues, it just means that he's moved from being 'that horrible man' to being simply the father of my children.

"Yes, I still get angry over things he does (or doesn't do), but I know that my fight is in the spirit and not with him. Yes, he still works at undermining my relationship with our kids, but I know God is bigger than that.

"I keep my boundaries, both physical *and* emotional. His actions don't rock me at the core anymore. I'll get mad, but now I pray and forgive very quickly. Plus, I pray for laborers to cross his path, and for him to be blessed.

"I knew from the beginning that in order not to become a bitter woman, I had to forgive. It was a choice I made. And it's been so worth it. I am free."

When Your Expectations Are Violated

So many situations of unforgiveness come up when our expectations are violated. We expect people to keep their word to us, and then they break it. We expect someone to help us, and they bail. We expect someone to have our back, and they betray us. We expect someone to protect us or treat us fairly, and they don't. We expect more from Christians and ministers, then they turn out to be very human and they disappoint us.

The list goes on and on. There's nothing that leads to unforgiveness faster than violated expectancies.

The Smith's Story: I knew a couple once — let's call them Ron and Brenda Smith — who wanted more than anything to go to Bible school. They served in helps ministry in their church, but they felt called to other areas of ministry too, and they wanted more training.

So they prayed and believed God for a way to go to the same out-of-state Bible school their pastor had gone to. But it looked like they would never be able to afford it.

Then one day, their pastor told them the church would pay their tuition to go that Bible school. Ron and Brenda were so excited! They made all the arrangements, loaded up all their belongings, put their two kids in the car, and drove the 2,000 miles to the Bible school. They had such a great time that first year, and their lives were impacted in a powerful way.

But at the end of that first year, they were contacted by their church back home. It turned out that some extenuating circumstances had happened, and the church simply would not be able to pay the tuition for the Smith's second year at Bible school.

The Smiths felt hurt and betrayed by their church. Their expectation had been violated and they were so disappointed! Rather than looking to God to provide, they focused on how the church had let them down. Within a couple weeks, they packed up their belongings and moved back home, giving up their dream of finishing Bible school. They didn't even return to church because they were so angry.

As far as I know, they're still bitter about it today, over 20 years later. They still blame that pastor and the church for the plan of their life getting derailed.

When I heard what happened, I felt so bad! I realize that the church let the Smiths down, but how tragic that they chose bitterness and disappointment over forgiveness and the pursuit of their dream. They expected one thing, got another, and they threw down their faith. I wanted to tell them, "God is your source! Forgive the church and look to him to provide. Hold onto your dream!"

So many times I think we are so hurt when our expectations get violated that we forget who our real source is and how he wants to meet every need in our life. Where God guides, he provides! I'm convinced this family was supposed to be at Bible school, and I'm so sad they succumbed to the plot of the devil and gave up their dream just because one source of provision dried up.

Don't let that be you! Remember, in spite of your expectations, people don't owe you anything. Look to God! He's the One who won't let you down. Hold onto your dream, no matter how many disappointments come along. There are bound to be all sorts of these bumps in the road as you pursue what's on your heart, but don't let them deter you.

*In spite of your expectations,
people don't owe you anything. Look to God!*

Determine to be a person who forgives quickly and moves on, looking to God to meet your needs not anyone else. Philippians 4:19 says, "And my God shall supply all your need according to his riches in glory by Christ Jesus." There's no one else who can supply your *every* need. Your Heavenly Father is a better provider than any human source. He'll never leave you or forsake you!

When one source dries up — when one expectation turns out differently — forgive and expect to see God move some other way on your behalf. If you'll continue to trust him, he knows how to make every disappointment turn out well for you (Rom. 8:28).

No More Power

One day while I was meditating on forgiveness, the Lord showed me that holding onto unforgiveness is like renting out property in your heart to someone (or something) that has hurt you. The more you think about it, the more property it consumes, until your heart is taken over by the poison, and it becomes hardened to the blessings of God. You don't want that!

Why would we choose to rehearse the pain or shame and give someone who hurt us any more power over our lives? Let's not give them any more airtime in our brain. Instead let's use that airtime to meditate God's Word or dream about our bright future in him! When we hold a grudge, we are prisoners of pain, giving those who have hurt us way too much power over our lives.

When we hold a grudge, we are prisoners of pain.

Don't let that happen! When you drag the pain of horrible people or events into your future, you become a victim, relinquishing the power to someone else. If you choose to hang onto bitterness and unforgiveness, no one suffers but you. It can cause you to lose your peace, your joy, and even your health. It's not worth it.

When you choose forgiveness, you are saying to that hurtful person or event, "No more power!" You are cutting the chain to the painful past and walking away. Forgiveness can give you back your joy, your peace, and your dignity.

It All Boils Down to This

Here's what I've learned in years of working with people: there will never be two people anywhere — much less two families, two churches, two states or even two nations — who agree on absolutely everything. There will always come a time when people disagree with one another; when someone misunderstands the intentions of another; when someone hurts us (or we hurt them); when people flat out want their own way and don't care who they tromp over to get it.

So you and I are going to have to spend our whole lives forgiving. We might as well get used to it, and we might as well get good at it!

We're going to have to spend our whole lives forgiving. We might as well get good at it!

How do we do that? What's the answer to fulfilling a lifetime of forgiveness? Thankfully, there *is* an answer. Jesus gave it to us when he came to earth with *one* commandment he wanted us to follow: "A new commandment I give to you, that you love one another; as I have loved you, that you also love one another" (John 13:34).

Simple, huh? Just one commandment! That's the only way it's possible to love one another, with his love; that same love he put into our hearts when we got saved (Rom. 5:5). *Agape* love, the same love with which he loves us. It's not natural human love; it's unconditional love that isn't based on earning or deserving. It's based on his goodness. We humans don't have the capacity to love this way on our own, and thankfully, we don't have to. We just have to yield to the love that God has put into our hearts by forgiving and letting him love others through us.

After Jesus told us this one commandment, he followed up by showing us just how powerful it is to love others the way he loves us: "By this all men will know that you are My disciples, if you have love for one another" (John 13:15).

According to Jesus, loving each other (which of course includes forgiving each other) is our witness before the world. Our witness is not our beautiful multi-purpose church buildings, or our dynamic sermons or amazing worship music complete with lights and smoke. It's not our outreaches, or our bumper stickers or lit-up nativity scenes in the front yard. Those things are all well and good, but it's love that the world is looking for. They're watching to see how well we love one another. This is our witness to the world.

If we only love the people who agree with us and love us back, we don't understand agape love yet. Luke 6:33 says, "If you do good to those who do good to you, what credit is that to you? For even sinners do the same." Agape love is the God-kind of love, or you could say it's the way God loves —unconditionally. This is where the real power and freedom lies in life.

If we only love the people who agree with us and love us back, we don't understand agape love yet.

First Corinthians 13 gives us the blueprint for walking in this agape love. In my own family we have memorized these four verses and endeavored to walk them out every day of our lives. I love it in the classic edition of the Amplified Bible:

Love endures long and is patient and kind; love never is envious nor boils over with jealousy, is not boastful or vainglorious, does not display itself haughtily.

5 It is not conceited (arrogant and inflated with pride); it is not rude (unmannerly) and does not act unbecomingly. Love (God's love in us) does not insist on its own rights or its own way, for it is not self-seeking; it is not touchy or fretful or resentful; it takes no account of the evil done to it [it pays no attention to a suffered wrong].

6 It does not rejoice at injustice and unrighteousness, but rejoices when right and truth prevail.

7 Love bears up under anything and everything that comes, is ever ready to believe the best of every person, its hopes are fadeless under all circumstances, and it endures everything [without weakening].

8 Love never fails . . . .

Because this is how God loves *me* (thank you, Lord!) and how he loves you, it's also how we can choose to love others. What would happen if we walked this out every day of our lives? What if we were patient and kind to everyone, whether they deserved it or not? What if we didn't insist on having things our way? What if we weren't touchy or fretful? What if we didn't pay *any attention at all* when someone wronged us? I think we would be walking on the victory side of life every single day.

I'm so thankful that God has given us instructions! Because this is not natural human love. We can't do this in our own strength. But we have supernatural help to walk in this kind of love. It's available to us every day!

I encourage you to meditate on 1 Corinthians 13: 4–8 until it seems more real to you than the pain of unforgiveness. Love and forgiveness are so very tied to each other. Really, forgiveness boils down to walking in agape love (the God kind of love). I can't choose to walk in love with someone but still hold a grudge against them. By the same token, I can't truly forgive someone without God's love flowing to and through me!

Thankfully, he has put his agape love on the inside of me — all I have to do is tap into it. All I have to do is want to, and ask God to help me. It's all you have to do, too.

Questions for Reflection and Discussion >>

• What is the crazy-cycle?

• What does it feel like when you can't forgive?

• Has there ever been a time in your life when you had to confront someone who had done you wrong? Had you forgiven them before confronting? What happened? Have you forgiven them now?

• Before reading this chapter, did you think forgiveness required a face-to-face or allowing someone who's been hurtful back into your life? What did you learn after reading?

········· Chapter 3 ·········

Setting the Captive Free

Let's take this idea of forgiving those who have hurt us one step farther. Could it be that forgiveness not only sets *us* free, but it can set free the one we're forgiving too? Read on.

Janie's Story: One term at Bible school, the forgiveness lesson I always taught in class happened to fall on a Friday. The following Monday after school, one of the students from that class — let's call her Janie — poked her head in my office door and said, "Ms. Karen, can I tell you a story that happened after I heard your lesson on forgiveness?"

Of course I wanted to hear it!

Janie came in, sat down, and proceeded to tell me her story. She explained that before she came to Bible school, she had been a student at a university. Actually, Janie confided that God had called her to the ministry and to Bible school, but she was running away from that plan, so basically, she was out of God's will being at that university. (That's another subject for another book, but it's worth mentioning that running away from God is never a good idea, and can get you into all sorts of trouble!)

One day during Janie's freshman year, she accepted a young man's invitation to go out on a date. Tragically, at the end of that date, the young man tried to rape her. Thankfully, she got away and wasn't physically harmed, but the episode shook her up very badly. Ever since it happened she'd been jumpy and fearful, she cried often, she couldn't sleep; it had even started affecting her health.

Not long after, Janie left the university, went to Bible school, and heard my lesson on forgiveness. At the end of that class, I always give students an opportunity to put into practice what was taught, just as I did at that ladies retreat. We took the time to write the name(s) of the person we needed to forgive in our Bibles, and prayed over them.

Janie realized that she needed to forgive this young man who had tried to rape her, so with a heart full of faith (from having heard the Word) she wrote his name in her Bible and prayed to forgive him.

"After I prayed to forgive him, I felt so free!"

"After I prayed to forgive him, I felt so free!" she told me with a smile. "I slept well that night and just noticed a sense of peace in my heart that had been missing for so long." I rejoiced with her! There's really nothing more satisfying for a teacher than to hear someone put into practice what's been taught, and to have it work in their lives. God is so faithful to perform his Word.

"But wait, Miss Karen, that's not all!" she said, her eyes wide. "The story gets much better!" I couldn't imagine how it could be even better than that.

The Rest of the Story

Janie proceeded to tell me that after her peaceful night's sleep, she woke up on Saturday morning and her phone rang. The caller I.D.

didn't show a name, but the area code of the caller was from Janie's home state, so she answered it.

After she said, "Hello," she heard a man's voice say, "You prayed for me." Janie realized right away that, out of the blue, *it was the young man who had tried to rape her.*

You have to realize that it had been over a year since the incident, and Janie had had absolutely no contact with the young man since that night. She told me, "If I'd known it was him calling, of course I never would have answered it."

She wanted to hang up, but he said it again, "You prayed for me." So she asked him what he meant, and he proceeded to tell her.

Apparently, the night before (the very same day Janie had forgiven him), he had been in a terrible car accident. Paramedics managed to keep him alive, an ambulance took him to the hospital, and after emergency care he was checked into ICU. Not long after he was admitted, he was alone in his hospital bed and he said he heard a voice (you have to remember that this young man was *not* a Christian. But guess what? God can make Himself heard by anyone he wants to! I love that about him).

The voice said to him, "You are alive because Janie forgave you."

Wait. What?! I have to say that when Janie told me that part of the story, I stared at her for a full 10 seconds with my mouth open! Could it really be that forgiveness not only set Janie free, but set the young man free too?

The answer is yes! Now just think about that for a minute. What are the far-reaching ramifications of our choice to forgive? Or even — and this is a chilling thought — of our choice to *not* forgive.

What are the far-reaching ramifications of our choice to forgive?

Janie's story ended in the best way possible. She was able to pray with her attacker over the phone, and he received Jesus as his savior.

He met God in a very real, very life-saving way when Janie forgave him, and as a result, his destiny has been changed forever.

"I Forgive You, But I Don't Want You To Be Blessed!"

Now let's be honest. There might be some of you who read Janie's story and thought, "I don't *want* the person who hurt me to be forgiven or get saved! That's the *last* person I want to get blessed!" I understand, I really do. But all I can say to that is, if you're thinking that way, quit it! That's your flesh, pure and simple, not your spirit, and there's no freedom there — for them *or* for you.

Here's the thing: you and I have been forgiven much. The Bible says that it is required of us then, as the forgiven, to forgive. Colossians 3:13 says, "Remember, the Lord forgave you, so you must forgive others" (TLB).

....

You and I have been forgiven much. It is required of us then, as the forgiven, to forgive.

....

Matthew 6 puts it another way in the Lord's prayer, which I'm sure you're familiar with: "Our Father which art in heaven, Hallowed be thy name. Thy kingdom come, Thy will be done in earth, as it is in heaven. Give us this day our daily bread. *And forgive us our debts, as we forgive our debtors*" (vv. 9–12). You could say, "The *way* you forgive is the same way you will be forgiven."

Would you like to be forgiven when you've made a mistake? Then forgive others when they make a mistake. Would you like to be forgiven quickly? Then forgive quickly. Would you like to be forgiven without conditions? Then forgive without conditions. The Bible says that you will be forgiven the same way that you forgive.

I don't know about you but I want all the mercy I can get. That requires that I give mercy to others.

We've Been Forgiven Everything

One of my favorite Bible examples about forgiveness is the parable Jesus tells in Matthew 18. He goes so far as to say that this story is what the kingdom of heaven is like. I think that makes it a pretty important point! And of course, it's about forgiveness:

> Therefore the kingdom of heaven is like a certain king who wanted to settle accounts with his servants. [24] And when he had begun to settle accounts, one was brought to him who owed him ten thousand talents. [25] But as he was not able to pay, his master commanded that he be sold, with his wife and children and all that he had, and that payment be made. [26] The servant therefore fell down before him, saying, "Master, have patience with me, and I will pay you all." [27] Then the master of that servant was moved with compassion, released him, and forgave him the debt.
>
> Matt. 18:23–27

So here we have a king who is looking at his financial affairs, and he wants to talk to all the people who owe him money. He calls in one particular servant who owes him — let's call it $10,000.00. The guy doesn't have the money and can't pay it back. It was a desperate situation because without the money, he was going to lose everything he had, plus he and his whole family were going to be sold into slavery to pay it back.

Naturally, the servant did what we all would probably do in that situation; he begged for mercy. And amazingly, the king not only released him instead of enslaving him, but he *forgave* the entire $10,000.00 debt.

....

The king not only released him instead of enslaving him,
but he forgave the entire debt.

....

Think about that! The king didn't reduce the amount the guy owed, or make a payment arrangement for him. He *erased* the debt completely. This servant didn't get what he deserved at all. That's a reason to celebrate! But sadly, that's not what this servant did. Read on.

> But that servant went out and found one of his fellow servants who owed him a hundred denarii; and he laid hands on him and took him by the throat, saying, "Pay me what you owe!" [29] So his fellow servant fell down at his feet and begged him, saying, "Have patience with me, and I will pay you all." [30] And he would not, but went and threw him into prison till he should pay the debt.

> vv. 28–30

His fellow servant owed him a fraction of what he himself had owed — let's say $100.00, compared to his former bill of $10,000.00. This ungrateful guy demanded that payment be made, to the point of *choking* his fellow servant. Notice that the words his fellow servant used; they are exactly the same ones he had used when the king demanded payment: "Have patience with me, and I will pay you all." But while his debt was forgiven, he completely ignored them when his fellow servant used them, and had the guy thrown into prison.

Well, when everybody else in the household heard about it, they recognized how unfair it was, and they told the king.

> So when his fellow servants saw what had been done, they were very grieved, and came and told their master all that had been done. [32] Then his master, after he had called him, said to him, "You wicked servant! I forgave you all that debt because you begged me. [33] Should you not also have had compassion on your fellow servant, just as I had pity on you?" [34] And his master was angry, and delivered him to the torturers until he

should pay all that was due to him. ³⁵ So My heavenly Father also will do to you if each of you, from his heart, does not forgive his brother his trespasses.

vv. 31–35

That last verse is sobering, don't you think? In the story, the ungrateful servant represents you and me. We have been forgiven everything by our King when we didn't deserve it. Our debt has completely been wiped out by Jesus. Should we not also have compassion on our fellow humans, just as he had pity on us? If we demand that payment be made, we would have to pay too, and it's a debt we cannot pay.

You and I simply have no right to hold anything against anyone since we have been forgiven everything. *Everything!* I don't know about you, but that makes it easier for me to forgive others. Plus, there's this added benefit. When I forgive them, it can also set *them* free.

That's amazing. And it doesn't seem to be an isolated incident. Here's another example.

They Both Got Free

Bethany's Story: "When I was a kid, my brother sexually abused me for over a year. As a result, I had nightmares and flashbacks all the time as I grew older. They tormented me. I was afraid of my brother, obviously, and even more so as we became teenagers and he became an alcoholic.

"I had heard about forgiveness, but I wasn't at all sure what it did or how to even do it. Then one day a mentor explained to me about the power of forgiveness and how Jesus had forgiven us for everything we ever did and ever would do. She told me forgiving my brother could set me free from the torment I was experiencing.

"That was amazing to me. I wasn't sure how to do that, but I wanted to! She helped me pray a prayer of forgiveness for what my brother had done to me. I prayed something simple like, 'God I choose to forgive my brother for sexually abusing me. I repent for harboring the anger and unforgiveness for so long and I give it all to you.' At the time I remember thinking, 'Sweet! This is it! I won't have to deal with the nightmares or the flashbacks or the fear anymore.'

"But that's not what happened. The very first night after I prayed, all those feelings came back! I thought maybe I hadn't really forgiven him. So I contacted my mentor and she told me that sometimes you have to forgive a person several times. She explained that it's like an onion where each time you forgive someone you're getting another layer of healing. So I kept at it and was determined to not let unforgiveness take hold in my heart.

"I was determined to not let unforgiveness take hold in my heart."

"One night specifically I remember praying about the situation and felt a deep relief in my heart. I didn't speak of it to anyone, just to make sure it was really God and had really worked.

"But the peace remained, *and* within two months of that night my alcoholic, drug-addicted brother was sober and making a better life for himself. As far as I know, he quit cold turkey. He just lost the desire and the need to drink. He got married this last summer and is the father to two wonderful kids.

"Do I think he got delivered the night I was finally able to forgive him? Well, that's between him and God, but you have to admit, it's quite a coincidence. All I know is that forgiveness brought freedom to me *and* to him."

I love this story! It's like a BOGO sale (Buy One Get One Free): forgiveness can set *everyone* free! When we choose to forgive, we receive peace and freedom, but it's also like turning someone over to the Lord, which enables him to work in them and turn entire situations around. What a powerful miracle.

When I hear stories like the ones in this chapter, I just want to tell everyone about the power of forgiveness. I want to help us all to realize that it's something we're going to have to be vigilant about all our lives.

As I've said before, we might as well get good at this, because there will always be opportunity to forgive.

Luke 17:1 and Matthew 18:7 say that offense is sure to come to all of us. It's inevitable! There are opportunities every single day to forgive someone. And when we do, we open the door to all sorts of miracles, both for ourselves and for the ones we're forgiving!

Questions for Reflection and Discussion >>

- Why do you think the servant who had been forgiven didn't forgive his fellow servant?
- What happened to the servant who didn't forgive his fellow servant?
- What do you think it means to be delivered to the torturers?
- What does that mean for us if we don't forgive?
- What has helped you the most so far in this book?

Chapter 4

When They Hurt Someone You Love

I know a lot of us feel it's easier to forgive a person who has hurt *us* than it is to forgive a person who has hurt someone we love one. We say, "Do anything you want to *me*, but when you hurt someone I care about, watch out!" If that's been you, read on.

> *Do anything you want to me, but when you hurt someone I care about, watch out!*

Rose's Story: I once heard about a young woman — let's call her Rose — whose father was brutally murdered one night by two men in a parking lot. I wrote about her story of forgiveness in my first book, *Why God Why? What To Do When Life Doesn't Make Sense*, and it helped so many people, I wanted to include it here too.

The two men who beat Rose's father to death were caught and arrested. One was sentenced to life in prison with the possibility of parole; the other went to death row.

Even though she was a Christian, Rose's heart was filled with hatred and bitterness toward the men who had senselessly killed her father. As time went by, the one man sentenced to death row died. But in a strange twist, 14 years after her father was killed, Rose had the opportunity to meet the other man who was serving a life sentence.

All during those years, God was dealing with Rose, softening her heart. She knew that Psalm 103 says that God "does not punish us as we deserve or repay us according to our sins and wrongs" (v. 10 GNT). She knew she couldn't change the past, and she couldn't control what other people had done, but she *could* control her response. She could leave the hurts and anger of the past behind when she chose to forgive. She knew God doesn't give us what we deserve or repay us according to our failures, so she didn't want to do that with anyone else.

When the opportunity came to visit her father's murderer in prison, she knew she had a choice to make. She didn't exactly know what she would say when she was face-to-face with him, but she planned at least to ask if he knew Jesus as his Savior.

Meanwhile during his time in prison, this man who had taken part in murdering her father had accepted the Lord. As a result, he stopped using drugs, and joined a prison job-retraining program. He felt terrible about having killed someone and had prayed the Lord would give him a chance to tell the family of his remorse.

Peace and Freedom

On the day that Rose went to the prison, both she and her father's killer were nervous. As they faced each other across the visiting cubicle, the man began telling Rose how sorry he was for what had happened. As he talked, the Holy Spirit began to move on Rose, and she felt prompted to tell the man she forgave him. And something miraculous happened. As soon as she said the words, "I forgive you," she could literally see something lift off of him, as if a huge burden was just gone. His face became lighter, and tears came to his eyes as he thanked her.

Even more miraculously, it wasn't until later that Rose realized the same thing had happened to her! When she forgave her father's killer and released him from his terrible guilt, she herself was also released from all the anger and bitterness she'd been carrying around inside of her. She felt a peace and a freedom she hadn't felt in all the years since her had father died. It was almost as if she were weightless.

Sometimes forgiving is like doing physical therapy. When a person goes through therapy on a wounded limb, it hurts to move that limb around and exercise it. And sometimes because it hurts, the person wants to stop because they don't want to deal with the pain. But you and I both know that if they stop, the limb won't get better.

In the same way, if we draw back from forgiving, our own heart can't get better. As soon as we choose to release the hurt, let it go, and forgive, our heart can receive the healing and restoration it needs. I like what one minister says: "Forgiveness is unlocking the door to set someone free and realizing you were the prisoner."

Forgiveness is unlocking the door to set someone free and realizing you were the prisoner.

If Rose could forgive what had happened to her father, you and I can forgive! Just like her, you can't change the past, *especially* if other people are involved. You can't control what other people do, but you *can* control your response. You can leave the hurts and anger of the past behind when you choose to forgive.

So Angry

Gloria's Story: Once I was ministering on forgiveness in a church and after the service a woman — let's call her Gloria — came up to talk with me. She told me that her son had been killed in the war in Afghanistan, and in her pain she not only mourned the loss of her son, but she was *so angry*.

Immediately I hugged her and held her tight. I have sons, and I have never had to send either one of them off to war. I can't even imagine how hard that is, and the pain of losing them in the line of duty. That much pain is unthinkable. I know that many, many mothers and families have experienced it, as well as families of those who serve as policemen, firemen, and other heroes. My heart goes out to all of them.

Gloria was grateful for my hug, but she wanted to explain what had happened as she listened to the Word I preached that morning. As I spoke, she realized that her anger was really unforgiveness. In the aftermath of her son's death, she was angry at the U.S. Army for putting her son in harm's way, she was angry at the U.S. president and congress for agreeing to war, and she *hated* Afghanistan — its people, its rulers, and especially its army.

I felt so bad for her. Imagine harboring unforgiveness against people you will never know or see. Against entire armies, nations and people groups! While I can understand Gloria's feelings, I'm so glad she realized her anger and unforgiveness were not hurting anyone but herself. There's no way to get restitution or an apology from all those people. They were mostly just nameless, faceless enemies in her mind, holding her hostage to her grief and pain.

Thankfully, hearing the Word of God showed Gloria what was really happening in her heart and mind, and it showed her the way to freedom. I could tell from talking to her that she was greatly relieved. She had prayed the prayer I always lead at the end of a service about forgiveness, and now there was a light in her eyes that I can imagine had not been there in a while. She had been able to forgive, and now she was free.

"I Forgive You, But Someone Has to Pay!"

When a loved one (or anyone we care about) has been hurt, we're very likely to think, "Someone has to pay!" We want judgement. We want those who have done the hurting to feel the same pain that they've caused, or worse.

But the truth is someone already *has* paid. Jesus paid for your sin, and the sin of those who have hurt you and your loved one. He who knew no sin was made to be sin for us (2 Cor. 5:21). First Peter 3:18 says, "For Christ also suffered once for sins, the just for the unjust, that he might bring us to God."

....

Someone already has paid.

....

There's no more payment for sin. It's all done. Hebrews 7:27 says, "This He did once for all when He offered up Himself."

When we're in covenant with Jesus, we don't live in a kingdom of paybacks; we live in a kingdom of mercy and grace. It's what we've all received.

I think of it this way: If *I* require judgement of someone who has done wrong, then I'm changing the rules from mercy and grace back to judgement. Then I must live under the rule of judgement as well.

And I don't want that. Neither do you.

James 2:13 says, "For judgment is without mercy to the one who has shown no mercy. Mercy triumphs over judgment." Read that again. Mercy triumphs over judgement! Let that get down into your spirit, so that you'll never again think someone has to pay. Someone already did.

Borrowed Offense

It's so easy to fall into offense on someone else's behalf and then harbor unforgiveness. Very often we don't even know we're doing it! We'll just hear a story about how someone was done wrong and then immediately jump on the bandwagon of how unfair that was and who's going to pay.

First, it's important to remember that there is always more than one side to the story. We hear a story of how someone was treated unfairly or hurt in some way, and we decide to take up their offense right along with them, but really we only know half the story.

....
There's always more than one side to the story.
....

It's so easy to fall into believing one side! It's one of the things I have learned as a minister. When you're counseling and listening to anyone talk, always remember there's more than one side to the story. I've lived it, I've taught it to others, and yet, I'm ashamed to say I've *still* fallen for it. I can still instantly get all wrapped up in what someone is telling me and want to jump on the bandwagon to defend them without stopping to realize I'm only hearing their side.

Nancy's Story (and mine too): I remember one time a friend — let's call her Nancy — told me how she was serving at the information booth at church when a well-known singer (who attended the church) came up to ask a question.

She said she answered him quickly and politely, but apparently he was short with her, just looked right through her, took the pamphlet she handed him, and walked off without saying thank you or acknowledging her in any way.

She was kind of miffed about it and after I heard her tell the story, I was kind of miffed about it too! I had always liked this singer's music and had listened to it a lot, but after she told me about that incident, I didn't enjoy his music as much. Every time I heard him sing, I'd think, "Man, he's not very nice to people." It ruined his music for me, and eventually I stopped listening.

One day I happened to hear one of his songs playing on the radio, and I started to turn it off (because I was still miffed at him) when the Lord arrested me. He spoke to my heart, saying, "You're offended. You're harboring unforgiveness against that man for something someone else told you." Then he got pretty plain with me. He said, "You weren't there, Karen and you don't really know what happened. And besides that, you don't know what that man was going through that day."

I was stunned. Oh my gosh, that was all true! I'd fallen into offense on behalf of my friend without even considering the other person's side. Besides that, I'd let it ruin my love for this singer's music. I'd believed the worst about him just from a story I'd heard.

The devil is so sneaky! I didn't even realize that I was harboring unforgiveness until the Lord pointed it out to me. I can tell you that it didn't take me long to repent and forgive. I did it right then and there in the car. Thankfully, I went back to enjoying that singer's music, and I also learned a valuable lesson about forgiving people who had hurt my friends.

Now I try to consider the other person's side, and I try not to believe the worst about someone from a story I've heard. I also try not to define someone by their worst moments. We all have bad moments. What if we were quick to forgive those and give people the benefit of the doubt?

I try not to define someone by their worst moments.

Taking on someone else's unforgiveness is a trap, pure and simple. Keeping our own hearts free and our own blessing pipe clear is a big enough job for anyone without taking on someone else's offense!

When Others Are Hurting

Elaine's Story: I have another friend — let's call her Elaine — who realized she was also harboring unforgiveness on behalf of others, and it started to affect her own life. She had several different friends in ministry who were treated badly, and it all happened within a short period of time.

It's just like the devil, isn't it, to pile things on? He can make you feel like *everyone* is being wronged everywhere you turn.

It's just like the devil, isn't it, to pile things on?

First, Elaine's prayer partner and her husband moved from one state to another to be youth ministers at a church. They became very successful and grew their youth group larger than the church. But they were treated badly. There were promises broken, the pastor had an affair and was fired, then they were passed over for the pastorate in spite of the people's wishes, and eventually the board let them go without severance pay (even though the adulterating pastor got severance!). Elaine walked through the whole ordeal with them, praying and believing God to the end. Today this couple is separated, living in different states and neither one are walking with God.

Next, Elaine knew a young man who was a youth pastor at a church where the pastor mentored him and they were best friends. The young man and his wife had their first child, quickly followed by a second, and then his wife had an affair with the pastor. It turned out that the pastor had had a previous moral failure, and even claimed that God told him to do it. This young couple is now divorced and neither of them are walking with God.

Elaine also knew a young girl who married a guy who was a great worship leader. They had a bad experience at the first church they worked at, left there and had another bad experience at the next church, all through no fault of their own. Now they are divorced and the young man is not following God.

Elaine was heartbroken. "I was so disappointed for each of these couples," she said. "They were trying to serve God and just do the right thing, and as far as I could see, they were. The people who were supposed to love them and nurture them did anything but. I knew God wasn't the one who did these people wrong, nor did he condone it.

"As a result of all this, I started having a really hard time trusting any authority in church. I loved God, but didn't like church at all."

Elaine and her husband left one church and tried several others, but couldn't seem to find one they liked. She had been a teacher in church before this, but now she wasn't serving, and every time they tried a new church she just kept waiting for the pastor or other leaders to show their "true colors" of hypocrisy or abuse.

Finally she was able to forgive the pastors and church leaders who hurt her friends, but it wasn't easy. "I'd get on the phone with my friends who'd been hurt, and after trying to encourage them to keep going with God, I would hang up so mad that I'm sure my blood pressure was up 50 points."

But the Lord kept telling her the same thing she was telling them: if she didn't forgive those pastors and leaders, she was just as wrong as they were for doing it. "I had to bring my emotions and thinking in line with my act of faith in forgiving them," she said. "Thank God for the Word that I had learned, and the Holy Spirit leading me through it all."

Collateral Damage

Today Elaine and her husband have found a church they love, and she is back to serving and teaching. Do you think it had anything to do with forgiving those who hurt her friends? I do. I believe that if she had continued to carry that offense, it would have vastly affected her own life in a negative way, and she may never again have gone to church steadily or served using her gifting.

It's a dangerous thing to harbor unforgiveness on the behalf of others. The devil works overtime to steal, kill and destroy, but he's overjoyed when the damage he does in one person's life spills over into someone else's. And that's just what happens when we become offended and hurt on behalf of someone else.

The devil is overjoyed when the damage he does in one person's life spills over into someone else's.

That's what we call *collateral damage*. Merriam-Webster's dictionary defines collateral damage as "injury inflicted on something other than an intended target." It's a military term, like when a bomb is dropped on a munitions storage facility but accidentally kills or injures civilians in the process. Those civilians were collateral damage. They were killed or injured by the bomb even though they weren't the intended target.

You can totally see how the term applies in taking on someone else's offense. The things that happened to Elaine's friends didn't happen to her, but the effects of the hurt started working in her life just as much as it did theirs. She was unhappy in church, she expected the worst from pastors and leaders, and she stopped serving. Her world was totally colored by the hurt she felt for her friends, and it was damaging her own life. The devil was pleased that his stealing, killing, and destroying efforts slopped over onto Elaine, even though she wasn't the intended target.

Thankfully, Elaine chose to dig into the Word of God and listen to his gentle promptings, and she was able to forgive. It's always a choice. She could have chosen to continue thinking about the terrible injustices that had been perpetrated against her friends. She could have let her mind dwell on the terrible results of their hurt — marriages destroyed, people walking away from God.

Instead, she "brought her emotions and thinking in line with her act of faith to forgive." It isn't easy. But it's vital. I think it's something we all have to check up on in our lives: "Am I offended on behalf of someone else?" If the answer is yes, stop the collateral damage right now and choose to forgive.

Mama Bear Syndrome

If you have children, you know that probably the hardest forgiving of all comes when someone hurts them. We can get what I call "Mama Bear Syndrome" (even though men can get it too). Mama Bears are well-known for being crazy-protective and coming to the rescue of their cubs when something or someone threatens them. Anyone who has any wilderness skills at all knows better than to mess with baby bear cubs in the woods, because if you come anywhere near them, you're going to incur the wrath of Mama Bear. She's going to strike first and ask questions later.

Mama (and Dad, and even Grandma and Grandpa) humans are the same way. If you hurt their kids in any way, you're going to incur their wrath. They're going to strike hard and fast, and ask questions later (or maybe not even ask questions at all). Mama Bears always take their children's side and always vilify anyone who hurts their child in any way.

There are a couple of problems with Mama Bear syndrome. The first problem is that thing about two sides to every story. Too often we come swooping in ready to defend our kids, but there could be a *slight* possibility (okay, maybe even more than *slight*) that our kid caused it or might be in some way in the wrong. Or at the very least, we take on their offense and agree with them that the one who did the hurting is all to blame.

As parents, we shouldn't automatically shift into high gear when our child is hurt. We should do some investigating and find out what is really happening. If we give our children the idea that they can do no wrong or that people owe them, they will grow up selfish and entitled. Sometimes the problem really did start with them, and they need to be held accountable in order to grow up into responsible, well-adjusted adults.

....

If we give our children the idea that they can do no wrong or that people owe them, they will grow up selfish and entitled.

....

If they really *are* victims of a terrible wrong, instead of a knee-jerk reaction, we can teach them to stand back and assess the situation in light of God's Word. We can help them see the other person's point of view — to walk a mile in their shoes, if you will. We can help them forgive, which will set them free. There will be no tolerance between people on earth if we don't teach this to our children. As parents, we can show them what God says about forgiveness and about his one commandment to love each other (John 13:34–35).

My Story: I remember when one of my sons was in elementary school, and he came home crying one day saying his teacher had yelled at him. The Mama Bear in me wanted to run immediately to that school and ream that teacher out for yelling at my precious boy. What in the world was she thinking, yelling at a little kid?

But instead, my son and I got out the Bible, read some scriptures, and we prayed for his teacher. We forgave her. I let him know that God was working in the situation for him, and that he could take comfort in that. He skipped away from our impromptu prayer meeting, tears gone, feeling much better.

I happened to be going to his classroom to volunteer the next day, and I asked the Lord for an opportunity to talk with his teacher about the yelling incident. Of course, he arranged the perfect time, and as I was sitting across from her cutting out stars, I just casually mentioned it.

Bless her heart, his teacher was horrified that she had hurt his feelings, and promised to try and speak more softly to him. She really didn't remember yelling at him at all.

The funny thing is, a few days later I was asking my son to do something, rather sternly I suppose, and he said, "Mom, you don't have to yell at me!" I was amazed. I hadn't yelled at him at all. But to his little ears, my stern tone obviously cut deep and he *felt* yelled at.

And I suddenly realized that something like that had probably happened with his teacher. She may have been speaking sternly, or she may have had a hundred other things going on at the same time (an elementary school teacher? Ya think?) and just spoken a little more loudly or harshly than she meant to.

What if I had stormed down to the school in full Mama Bear mode and taken her to task for "yelling" at my son? Proverbs 18:13 TLB says, "What a shame—yes, how stupid!—to decide before knowing the facts!" Yikes. I would have been stupid, plus I would have missed a learning opportunity for my son, and I would have wrongfully accused his teacher.

The Second Problem

The second problem with Mama Bear syndrome is that life is hard. It's inevitable that your child will be hurt at some point in their life, more than once. If you react immediately with "you poor baby!" and fly off to defend them against anyone and anything that has hurt them, all they learn is that Mama Bear will defend them. They don't learn anything about how to handle people, hurt, or adverse situations.

If we do everything for our kids — including defending them when they've been wronged — they'll never learn to stand on their own two feet, they'll never learn how to resolve conflict on their own (which is a very important life skill), and they'll never learn the power of forgiveness. They'll depend more on you than they do on God, and that is really handicapping them for life.

If we do everything for our kids, they'll never learn the power of forgiveness.

Sometimes we think we're helping them, but it's really hurting them to do everything for them. One of the best examples I've ever seen of that is watching a baby chick hatch out of an egg. Have you ever seen that happen? It takes a *long* time, and at certain points you think that little chick just isn't going to do it. First comes the beak, pecking and pecking to make a hole, and pretty soon a wet little head is poking out of the shell, gasping for breath, panting like he's exhausted.

Then after he rests awhile with his head poking out, he starts to move around, grunting and shrugging, the egg rocking all around until — ah-ha! — out comes a wet, matted down wing. And the poor little chick stops again, panting. It's at this point you think he just isn't going to be able to do it. You want to reach down and break open that shell to help him.

A word of warning: don't do it! Because in the end, after a long struggle, the wet and weary chick manages to get completely free of the egg shell. As he stands there all gooey and wobbly, you think, "Man, I hope he makes it, he looks terrible after all that struggle." But if you were to come back within the hour, you wouldn't even recognize him. He's fluffy and yellow and eating up a storm! It's the same with every chick.

And here's the part I want you to know: if you had given into temptation while you were watching, and helped that little wet and weary chick break out of the shell, *he would have died*. It was painful to watch his struggle, but he needed every muscle he used to break out of that shell to be strengthened in such a way that insured his survival in the outside world.

Think about that for a moment in the context of our kids. I know we don't like to see them struggle, but that's how they learn. That's how they develop the "life lesson" muscles they'll need to survive and thrive. Obviously there are times we step in to help them, but be careful. Don't do everything for them. Instead, train them in childhood how to handle hurtful situations by leading them to God's Word and the power of forgiveness.

Truth Wins

And we do this by example! We can't harbor unforgiveness our-selves and then expect our kids to forgive. I like the way one of my Mama Bear friends chose to handle things when someone hurt her almost-grown child recently:

Linda's Story: "I have the hardest time forgiving those who hurt my children, and I've been walking that out this past year. I've found that what works for me is to just agree with the Word for the person who hurt them.

"Early on, there was nothing in me that even wanted to forgive. So I just started saying things like 'Lord, you want good for _____ (person's name) and I thank you for that.' Or 'Lord, you are a God of restoration and that is what you desire for _____.'

"I just spoke the Word and agreed with the Lord's heart for the person who had hurt my child. Even though it felt very fake at first, I knew it was *truth*, and truth always sets us free (John 8:32). It always wins. The Word is alive and powerful. It began to penetrate my heart and supernaturally change it. I still fight my flesh and my emotions, and sometimes I'm tempted to butt in, but I don't. I keep believing that truth wins."

The Way God Sees It

Joanie's Story: I have another friend — let's call her Joanie — who struggled to forgive her ex-daughter-in-law after she divorced Joanie's son, even though she was a Christian. I absolutely love the revelation God gave Joanie one day about forgiving this woman who had hurt her son so badly:

"I had struggled with forgiving my ex-daughter-in-law for a long time. One day I was reading an article about forgiveness, and suddenly I realized I had never taken the time to see *her* the same way God sees *me* — as his child. Even though I had made an effort to forgive her, I still carried in my mind the same ugly picture of her from years ago.

"So I felt led to pray for her and her future, and here's what came to me: She is a new creature in Christ, with no past. Old things have passed away, behold all things have become new in her life, and she is the righteousness of God in Christ (2 Cor. 5:17, 21). Jesus paid for her with his blood . Her sins and her past are just as wiped out as mine (1 John 1:7). She has a bright future just like me!

"Jesus paid for her with his blood. Her sins are just as wiped out as mine!"

"The Bible tells us to 'forget those things which are behind' (Phil. 4:14) and I realized that's not only what I'm supposed to do in my life, but in her life too! If God is for me (Rom. 8:31), he is also for her.

"God never gives up on anyone, so why would I? Jeremiah 29:11 is applicable to all Christians: "For I know the thoughts that I think toward you, says the LORD, thoughts of peace and not of evil, to give you a future and a hope." He's given her a future and a hope too.

"I would send a birthday gift to my ex-daughter-in-law every year, and even send Christmas breakfast to her house every year, but my words about her didn't always line up. Now I have a new attitude toward her, and really toward anyone I've struggled with. I wish I had gotten this revelation years ago. But it's a new day!"

It can be a new day for you and me too. We can apply those same scriptural principles to anyone who has hurt our loved ones, or anyone we have struggled to forgive. We can ask God to help us see them the way He does — with the same grace, mercy, and bright future as he sees us. That is the path to freedom!

Questions for Reflection and Discussion >>

• What did you think after reading Rose's story?

• Have you ever borrowed an offense? What happened? Would you do it differently now?

• Have you ever been a part of collateral damage? How can forgiveness help?

• Have you ever been a Mama Bear, or experienced someone who acted like one?

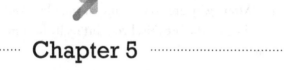

Chapter 5

Forgiveness and Physical Healing

Sheila's Story (part two): Remember Sheila from chapter 2, the lady from the retreat who forgave the cult leader and slept through the night for the first time in 20 years? Well, her story didn't end there! It turns out even *more* of her "blessing pipe" got unplugged when she was able to forgive.

After our testimony time that Saturday morning at the retreat, all of us ladies headed back into the city, and the next day I ministered at their church's Sunday morning service. As I was standing by my product table after the service that morning, Sheila came up to me and said, "Karen, you'll never guess what else happened."

Now, let me preface this next part by saying that at the retreat, Sheila had been what I would call a "loud talker." She just spoke several decibels above everyone else, even in a regular conversation. So when she came up to me on Sunday morning, I noticed right away that she was speaking much more quietly.

And apparently I wasn't the only one who noticed.

"When I got home from the retreat," she said, "my kids all asked me, 'Mom, why are you talking so quietly?' And I said, 'Well, I don't know! I guess before this, I couldn't really hear myself talking. But now I can hear perfectly.'"

Her wide eyes suddenly filled with tears as she said to me, "Karen, I believe I had a hearing loss, and then when I forgave, I got healed!"

That's when I learned that unforgiveness can hinder our healing. I'm not saying that's always the case, but I have heard many, many stories since then about people who received not only emotional and spiritual healing after they forgave, but they received physical healing as well.

Unforgiveness can hinder our healing.

That makes sense, because we see healing and forgiveness alongside each other many times in the Bible. For example Psalm 103:2–3 says, "Bless the Lord, O my soul, and forget not all his benefits: who forgives all your iniquities, who heals all your diseases." You can see the two benefits listed there together: forgiveness of our iniquities and healing of our sicknesses. It's obvious that healing *and* forgiveness go together. Healing is always God's will for us, and so is forgiveness.

"I Forgive You, But I Want You to Know
How Much You Hurt Me!"

Kathy's Story: One young woman — let's call her Kathy — told me a story that also links physical healing to forgiveness.

When Kathy was a little girl, she was regularly abused by her brother. As a result, she had nightmares well into adulthood. She was also, understandably, afraid of men in general, and of her brother in particular.

Kathy heard several sermons on forgiveness before she realized it was something she needed to do concerning her brother. But it was hard! She knew she should forgive, but all she could think of was the tremendous hurt her brother had inflicted upon her. It seemed like forgiving him would just be condoning what he'd done and letting him get away with it. She wanted him to know how much he had hurt her.

But Kathy persevered, and began studying the Bible in earnest on the topic of forgiveness. She finally realized that her brother may never understand the pain his actions caused, but that holding unforgiveness against him wasn't hurting him at all. It was hurting her.

"I can't point to the exact scripture that set me free," she says. "It was more an accumulation of all of them. But one day the truth just settled into my spirit. I knew I needed to forgive my brother."

"I knew I needed to forgive my brother."

When Kathy prayed and was able to finally forgive him, she says that she immediately felt free. The nightmares went away, the tormenting fear stopped, and she knew that she had cut that chain to her past. She said, "I became happier and wasn't depressed all the time."

Praise God, those changes alone would make this a wonderful testimony, but the story doesn't end there! Kathy also told me, "Before this. I used to get strep throat and ear infections (at the same time) almost every two or three months continuously. But since the moment I forgave my brother, I haven't had *either!*"

Getting into Position

So many times we don't recognize unforgiveness as a hindrance to our healing. I know I have been tempted to ask God, "What does *forgiveness* have to do with *healing?*" But the Bible clearly shows they are linked, and I have personally seen a lot of instances where they are related.

I've also seen study after study done by the medical community that reinforces the idea of forgiveness and healing. I have read that unforgiveness is actually classified in some medical books as a disease! According to Dr. Steven Standiford, chief of surgery at the Cancer Treatment Centers of America, refusing to forgive makes people sick and keeps them that way. With that in mind, forgiveness therapy is now being used to help treat diseases, such as cancer.[1]

Have you, or anyone you've known, had trouble getting healed, even though you've been believing God's Word for your complete recovery? It's not always caused by unforgiveness, but I think examining your heart for any unforgiveness is a great place to start.

Now don't misunderstand me, it's always God's will to heal us. In the Old Testament, he showed his people over and over that he is a healing God: "I am the Lord who heals you" (Ex. 15:26).

In the New Testament God solidified his covenant of healing through Jesus. Matthew 8:17 says "He Himself took our infirmities and bore our sicknesses" and 1 Peter 2:24 says, "Himself bore our sins in his own body on the tree, that we, having died to sins, might live for righteousness—by whose stripes you were healed." In God's mind, your healing was bought and paid for on the cross over 2,000 years ago. It's a done deal.

But as we've seen, unforgiveness is out of God's will for our lives. If we're holding a grudge, we've clogged our blessing pipe and we could be out of position to receive all our benefits in Christ. If God starts to prick our hearts about forgiving, he may well be trying to get us into position for physical healing.

If God starts to prick our hearts about forgiving, he may well be trying to get us into position for physical healing.

The Power to Forgive Is the Same Power That Heals

In Mark 2, Jesus was ministering in a house that was so full of people that a paralyzed man had to be lowered through the roof by four of his friends in order to reach him.

And their plan worked. "When Jesus saw their faith, he said to the paralytic, 'Son, your sins are forgiven you'" (Mark 2:5). But isn't that a funny way to heal someone? He didn't address the sick man's paralysis, instead he talked about sin. That didn't go over very well with the Jewish scribes who were there, either. They were thinking: "Why does this Man speak blasphemies like this? Who can forgive sins but God alone?" (v. 7).

And Jesus knew exactly what was on their minds.

> But immediately, when Jesus perceived in His spirit that they reasoned thus within themselves, He said to them, "Why do you reason about these things in your hearts? [9] Which is easier, to say to the paralytic, 'Your sins are forgiven you,' or to say, 'Arise, take up your bed and walk'? [10] But that you may know that the Son of Man has power on earth to forgive sins"—He said to the paralytic, [11] "I say to you, arise, take up your bed, and go to your house." [12] Immediately he arose, took up the bed, and went out in the presence of them all.
>
> vv. 8–12

Jesus was showing us that the power to forgive is the exact same power that heals. It's supernatural power! The Bible calls that power "anointing," the same spiritual force that Jesus talked about in Luke 4:18 when he said, "The Spirit of the Lord is upon Me, because He has anointed Me to preach the gospel to the poor; He has sent Me to heal the brokenhearted, to proclaim liberty to the captives and recovery of sight to the blind, to set at liberty those who are oppressed." The anointing to preach, heal, and proclaim liberty is also the power behind forgiveness.

It's plain to see that if we don't forgive, we could be blocking — or at the very least, hindering — God's healing anointing and keeping it from working in our lives. I know I don't want to do that! And I'm sure you don't either.

If we don't forgive, we could be hindering God's healing anointing and keeping it from working in our lives.

But what if someone has hurt us so much that we can't even stand the thought of them? What if we just keep thinking of it over and over? All we really have to do is obey Jesus. We don't have to try and "feel better" about the person who hurt us – forgiveness isn't about feelings. It's just an act of obedience – a choice.

So choosing to forgive is simply putting God's Word above our emotions and deciding to say, "I forgive." The faster we do that, the better. Instead of rehearsing thoughts of the hurt over and over, we can just do what God has commanded right away and forgive. That will keep the anointing — the power — flowing into our lives in every area, including healing.

The Medical Connection

As I mentioned earlier, even scientists and the medical community have discovered the power of forgiveness. Many doctors and scientists acknowledge there is a direct relationship between forgiveness and health. Studies have shown that holding onto anger or a grudge — harboring unforgiveness — can have very real, very devastating effects on our physical bodies.

Many doctors and scientists acknowledge there is a direct relationship between forgiveness and health.

The fact is that hurt, anger, loss, guilt, or envy, can profoundly affect the way our bodies function, and therefore affect our health. The very chemicals and electricity in our bodies are affected in a negative way. Unforgiveness can also disrupt brain waves, making us less able to think clearly and to make good decisions.

This scientific proof is just another reason that forgiveness is a good idea. I mean, is holding onto hurt really worth jeopardizing your own health? I say no! God knows what he's talking about when he commands us to forgive. He wants the best for you, spirit, soul and body.

Here are six things that can happen to our bodies if we harbor unforgiveness:

1) **It can hurt your heart.** Many times in this book when we've talked about your "heart," we've meant your *spiritual* heart, the heart of your inward being, the heart with which you believe (Rom. 10:10). But we're talking here about your actual, physical, blood-pumping heart. Holding onto anger and unforgiveness can take a serious toll. A study published by the American Heart Association shows that holding a grudge may increase your risk of coronary heart disease.[2] A report by Men's Health also showed that bottling up your anger instead of forgiving may increase your blood pressure.[3]

2) **It can affect your mental health.** Studies have shown that if we don't forgive, but rather let upsetting events and people stay in our minds, it can lead to anxiety, stress, and angry outbursts. One psychologist suggests that holding onto hostile emotions, instead of forgiving and letting them go, can manifest into physical problems.[4] Unforgiveness can also lead to depression; low self-esteem; depriving yourself of the good opportunities that life offers you; punishing yourself through activities or relationships that work out to harm yourself; addictions and so on.

3) **It can raise your blood pressure.** The psychology department at Hope College in Holland, Michigan, studied 35 women and 36 men who rehearsed hurtful memories and harbored unforgiveness, and found their skin, heart rate, and blood pressure were all affected negatively. Those negative effects lasted even into recovery periods (in other words, the effects lingered on and on in their bodies). When participants were encouraged to think forgiving thoughts,

they immediately felt more in control, and the tests showed their physical symptoms abated, including lower heart rate and blood pressure.[5]

4) **It can cause aches and pains in every muscle of your body.** Unforgiveness literally affects your muscular-skeletal system by increasing muscle tension and thereby producing headaches, joint pain/aches, stomachaches and ulcers, plus dizziness and tiredness, just to name a few. When you're angry or bitter, your muscles may tighten, which can cause imbalances or pain in your neck, back and limbs. There is also decreased blood flow to the joint surfaces, which makes it more difficult for the blood to remove wastes from the tissues.[6]

5) **It can hinder your sleep.** As we've seen, unforgiveness can keep you awake at night, which increases chances of delayed or inadequate repair to your body, done while you sleep. It can also cause your teeth to clench at night contributing to problems with your teeth and jaw joints. When you suffer from lack of sleep, the peptide and hormonal chemical "messengers" can be altered in every system of your body. The blood flow to your heart can be constricted. Your digestion can be impaired. One 2005 study showed that people who chose to forgive saw vastly improved sleep quality, among many other health benefits.[7]

6) **It can affect your children.** Young children are very susceptible to the emotions in their environment, and they are imitators. Do we want them to imitate our irritation, anger, and unforgiveness, or our mercy, compassion, and ability to forgive quickly?

It's no wonder that God commands us to forgive. He wants us to live happy, carefree, and *healthy* lives!

Healed of Hearing Loss

Mary's Story: Mary began to have hearing problems when she was just a little girl – it all started in first grade when she had German measles. That led to ear surgery in the third grade, and in seventh grade she had tubes put in her ears.

But in spite of all the medical intervention, Mary's hearing just got worse and worse as she grew up, and by the time she was an adult she was wearing hearing aids. She had more surgery, but still couldn't hear well, and she experienced discomfort as liquid and wax filled her ears daily. She said she would wake up in the morning feeling like she had slept in a swimming pool all night.

Meanwhile, in a seemingly unrelated vein, Mary was having troubles with someone she worked with. For more than a year and a half she and this person were at odds with each other.

"There were pop-up confrontations between us almost every day," said Mary. But then God dealt with her about forgiving her coworker, using the strategies we're talking about in this book, and she was able to do it, with help from the Bible.

Not long after Mary prayed and forgave her coworker, one of the pastoral staff members at her church came up to her out of the blue and asked if he could pray for her hearing. She had just received new hearing aids and was about to go back for an adjustment on them the following week.

The pastor had her take out the hearing aids, put his fingers in both her ears and prayed that her hearing be totally restored. Then he told her not to put the hearing aids back in for any reason. He said, "Go ahead and sell them on ebay, you'll never need them again!"

Mary said, "I stood on the words he told me, and I've been hearing without the hearing aids ever since!" Her ears no longer fill with liquid or wax, and when she went back to the hearing specialist to be tested, he said her hearing was in the normal range. "That was the first time I had *ever* been told that!" said Mary. "I am so very grateful to our Lord."

Do you suppose it was a coincidence that Mary forgave her coworker and almost right away her pastor approached her about praying for her hearing? I don't think so! I believe that as we line our lives up with God's principles, which always includes forgiveness, we put ourselves in position to receive all he has for us, and that includes physical healing.

....

As we line our lives up with God's principles, which always includes forgiveness, we put ourselves in position to receive all he has for us.

....

A Dream Fulfilled

Darleen's Story: This one is kind of funny and almost unbelievable – but true! It's about Darleen, whose dream was to sing on the platform in church, but she did not have a good singing voice. She often prayed about it, but it didn't seem like a prayer that could be answered; her voice just wasn't good enough to be heard in public.

Well one day, in a seemingly unrelated incident, Darleen felt the Lord instruct her to make a list of all the people in her life who had in some way wronged her – in other words, those people that she felt unforgiveness toward.

It took Darleen quite a while to make the list – it wasn't an easy task, and brought up some hurtful memories. But she obeyed, and when the list was complete, the Lord directed her to forgive them all. This was no five-minute thing. She spent time reading forgiveness scriptures in the Bible (like those we're reviewing in this book) and letting them soak into her spirit.

When she felt like she had faith to forgive, she prayed, and once and for all she forgave all those people on her list. Right away she felt freedom and peace as the weight of unforgiveness rolled off of her.

But then, not long after this, Darleen was doing some dusting around the house and began humming to herself. Pretty soon she was singing out loud. And she realized with a start that she sounded good!

She sang out loud for her husband when he came home, and they were both astonished to realize that all of a sudden, she had a beautiful singing voice. Long story short, she now sings in her church choir and often does solos.

Isn't God amazing? I wonder how many of us have dreams on our heart that aren't being fulfilled because our blessing pipe is clogged by unforgiveness? This particular story might sound a little crazy, but I believe forgiveness can put us into position for all sorts of God's blessings.

Questions for Reflection and Discussion >>

• Have you ever wanted someone to understand how much they've hurt you? What do you think now after reading this chapter?

• How do forgiveness and healing go together in the Bible?

• Have you experienced any of the ill effects listed here? Do you think it could be due to unforgiveness?

• How has knowing this connection helped you?

Chapter 6

Especially for Ministers

Hank's Story: This is a secondhand story, but such a good one that I told it every year in my class when I was a Bible school instructor. I think it illustrates such an important lesson for us all, especially those in ministry.

Once upon a time, there was a pastor — let's call him Hank — who had pioneered a church and poured his life into it. He preached multiple services every week, dedicated babies, baptized new believers, performed weddings and funerals, visited people in their homes and hospitals, helped his members deal with crises, counseled for hours, and even built most of the church's new building with his own hands.

Hank was completely dedicated to his congregation and gave of himself to them for many years.

One year, just after the new building was finished and the congregation had swelled to over 500 people, Christmas rolled around. On a Sunday in the middle of December, Hank and his wife were presented with a gift from the whole congregation. On the following Monday,

Hank called the national office of his ordaining organization (where I later worked and heard the story), and he wanted *out*.

"I quit!" he almost shouted over to the phone to one of the office staff ministers. "I have poured my life into this church, I even built most of the new building with my own hands! I've done everything for them! And do you know what a congregation of 500 people gave me and my wife for Christmas?!" The staff member could almost hear Hank's blood pressure going through the roof and his face turning beet red.

"They gave us a 5 x 7 picture of Jesus!" Hank hollered. "That's all that 500 people could put together to give us! How's that for appreciation? Not an 11 x 14 picture, not even an 8 x 10. Do you hear me? They gave us a 5 x 7 picture of Jesus! That's it, I quit. Get somebody else up here to take over this church. I don't have to stay where I'm not appreciated!"

When You Feel Unappreciated

Poor Pastor Hank! Everyone likes to be appreciated and thanked for their hard work. You can tell that he was very hurt by what he perceived as a terrible slight. And I'm sure he'd been thinking of nothing else since the Sunday morning service. He'd whipped himself into a pretty good frenzy, letting his thoughts run amuck.

Everyone likes to be appreciated and thanked for their hard work.

He probably even knew of some other pastors in similar-sized churches who had gotten cars or tropical vacations as Christmas gifts from their congregation. That just added fuel to his fire.

After Hank's outburst on the phone, the office staff minister had the great presence of mind to ask some really good questions. "Hank, tell me, why did you first go to that city to start a church?"

After a brief silence, Hank answered, "Because we felt God called us to." Then right on the heels of that declaration he started in again, "But I don't have to stay where I'm not appreciated! These people don't even know what they have, and they could care less about us! I'm quitting, get someone up here to take over!"

Then the staff minister asked him, "Hank, if God called you to start the church, has he told you to leave?"

As you might guess, there was no answer to that question. God hadn't instructed Hank to leave. He wanted to quit because he was offended and hurt and felt unappreciated.

Now, we've all felt like that at one time or another, especially those of us in the ministry. It seems like very often the people who you help the most are the ones who turn on you. Or at the very least, people just don't understand how hard you've worked or what it has cost you. It's so easy to fall into the trap of being offended, or feeling sorry for yourself, or being angry at people who don't appreciate you.

The good news from this story is that Pastor Hank didn't quit his church. The staff member was able to help him realign his perspective with God's Word. He forgave his congregation and got back to a place of serving God with joy.

Why We Serve God in Ministry

The important thing to remember when you're feeling unappreciated, offended or hurt by people (and therefore harboring unforgiveness) is that you don't serve in ministry to be appreciated by people.

Yes, if you're in the ministry, you're called to serve and bless people, but do it for the Lord, not for them. Because sometimes people *will* appreciate you — they should, and it's great when they do — but sometimes they won't! We can't let appreciation (or kudos or fame) be the reason we serve God.

Don't do what you do to be appreciated by people.

There's really only one reason to serve God in ministry: to obey him and his calling on our lives. As a minister, Hank's story helped me understand that I'm not in the ministry to please people. I do it to please God.

In fact, when I first heard this story I was a pastor and I told it to my own staff members. Then I gave them each their own 5x7 picture of Jesus! I wanted them to see it often and remember that they had better be doing what they did (serve in the church) to please God and no one else.

Colossians 3:17 puts it plainly: "And whatever you do in word or deed, do all in the name of the Lord Jesus, giving thanks to God the Father through Him." Then verse 23 seals the deal: "And whatever you do, do it heartily, as to the Lord and not to men."

Notice both of those verses say "whatever you do!" If you and I do *everything* we do every day in the name of Jesus — doing it *heartily* as if we were doing it for God and not for anyone else, and being *thankful* — I think we'll get it right. And we'll avoid the pain of feeling unappreciated.

If we work hard in ministry but people don't like it or appreciate it, we'll still be okay, because we're only aiming to please God. That is freedom! That's walking in a place of perpetual forgiveness, with all the blessings flowing.

Now, I know that sounds pretty simplistic, but when I got that truth down into my spirit, I started to live for an audience of one, and life got much sweeter. It has helped me to forgive people quickly and move on. It has set me free so I can keep my eyes on Jesus and my calling.

In Matthew 22:37, Jesus gives us the recipe for success in ministry: "You shall love the LORD your God with all your heart, with all your soul, and with all your mind."

I think it's good for ministers to check their heart once in a while. To ask themselves: "Am I doing what I do for approval? For appreciation or kudos or fame? For money or any reason other than pleasing

God?" If the answer is yes, it's simple to make the adjustment and remember why we do what we do.

Keep Bitterness at Bay

John's Story: I remember hearing one minister — let's call him John — share his own version of this truth. One time when John was very young and just starting out in ministry, he was privileged to spend time with an older, seasoned minister. This older minister was in his 80s by then, a dynamic preacher and a wonderful soul-winner who had helped start many churches around the world.

After spending some time around him, John approached the older minister and said, "Sir, you have been in ministry a long time, you've been very successful and learned many things. I'm just starting out. Is there anything you can tell me about how to be as successful in ministry as you've been? Any advice you can give me?"

The older man's eyes sparkled as he looked intently at John. "Just one thing, young man: if you can keep from getting bitter, you'll make it."

"If you can keep from getting bitter, you'll make it."

Wow. Just one thing. This wonderful minister of God had tapped into the one most important key for success and longevity in ministry: don't get bitter. That must mean there's a great potential for getting bitter! I'm sure every minister could agree that's true. So we must guard against it vigilantly.

Hebrews 12:15 warns us about bitterness: "See to it that no one fails to obtain the grace of God; that no "root of bitterness" springs up and causes trouble, and by it many become defiled" (ESV).

I'm sure this wise older minister would agree that the only way to keep from getting bitter is to forgive quickly and easily, even when someone does us wrong or doesn't appreciate us. Ephesians 4:31 says, "Let all bitterness...be put away from you."

God put that in the Bible because he knew there would be opportunities to get bitter. So don't fall for it! Put it away from you by forgiving! It takes practice, but keeping bitterness at bay by forgiving people quickly leads to a life of freedom and empowerment. It keeps anyone's — especially a minister's — blessing pipe flowing.

When People Leave

Tammy's Story. One pastor's wife — let's call her Tammy — told me a story that many pastors can relate to. Several years ago, one of their key staff members needed to be released from her position, and it went badly.

To complicate matters, the staff member and her family were very close to the pastor's family. For years they had done things together outside of the church, and had invested in each other's lives. Their kids were best friends, and Tammy and the staff member were especially close.

When Tammy and her pastor husband asked the staff member to step down, she took it very hard and was very angry. "My heart was so heavy," said Tammy. "I knew how badly it hurt her, but I also knew it absolutely the right thing for her, her family and the church."

Things got worse when the former staff member started talking badly about the pastors to other church members. As a result, many people began leaving. "We lost people that I seriously thought would *never* leave," said Tammy. "We had supported them when no one else would, and saw them through some very traumatic times in their lives. Yet they called my husband a manipulator and said I was a liar."

One day Tammy was at home, sitting in her recliner crying over the situation, and she really felt like quitting. "I said to myself, 'I don't have another 20 years of ministry in me. This is too hard! I would be perfectly happy going to someone else's church and being the best volunteer ever, but letting another pastor deal with all the heartache. I cried out, 'God, why have you called us to do this? I don't think I have it in me!'"

That's when God spoke to her heart and said, "You don't have it in you. But I have it in me. You are looking at ministry all wrong. You are not supposed to be doing it for you. You are supposed to be doing it for me."

....

"You don't have it in you. But I have it in me."

....

The Lord went on to remind Tammy that at the end of her life, she would be accountable for every idle word out of her mouth (Matt. 12:36). "He showed me how important it is to keep my heart and my words right," Tammy said, "So that I could stand before him one day and hear 'Well done, you kept your heart right, you kept your words pure, and you did it for Me.' "

Freer Than Ever Before

So Tammy chose to forgive those who were lying about her and making her life miserable. It took some time, and it was an effort to keep her thoughts in line with God's Word. "When you're going through persecution, it tries to consume your thoughts," she said, "so I had to continually remind myself of what God said. When thoughts about what people were saying came rushing into my mind, I immediately prayed for those people, reminding myself of what a great honor it is to serve God. I commanded those thoughts to bow" (2 Cor. 10:5).

"That totally took all the pressure off me!" she said. "I was free! Free to do the work that Jesus called me to. I realized that I'm not called to make everyone happy or to have everyone like me."

After she forgave, Tammy reported that her heart was filled with compassion for the former staff member and all the others who had left and told lies about her and her husband. Every time she thought of them now, she prayed for them.

"I am freer now than ever before," she says happily. "Because of the power of forgiveness, I can run into people that left our church years ago and have no reservations about going up to them and talking to them. They might be uncomfortable, but I have no offense, so I can genuinely ask them about their kids, their life, etc. It's funny: before I forgave, I was the one who would try to dodge them or go down a different aisle in the grocery store to avoid them. But now if I see *them* trying to avoid *me*, I wave real big and say hi!"

Forgiveness also gave Tammy a whole new perspective on ministry. "I'm not doing this for me, because it's not what I would choose," she says, "I'm doing it for God, because He called me. I do it because I love him and I want to serve him. This is a small sacrifice compared to what He did for us. Everyone didn't love Jesus either."

....

"I'm not doing this for me. I'm doing it for God."

....

"The Bible says that if you live a godly life, there will be persecution (2 Tim. 3:12). We don't really like that part, but we can walk victoriously through the trails and hard times! In John 16:33, Jesus says, "In the world you will have tribulation; but be of good cheer, I have overcome the world." When we lean on God and forgive, He is faithful to give us encouragement and strength in our weakness. In him we can overcome!"

Frustrated

Sam's Story: I knew a young man — let's call him Sam — who was called to ministry, but something seemed to be hindering him from really getting started. There was no doubt that he was called to do it. Sam had a powerful anointing to win souls, especially youth, and whenever he got the chance to preach, many people would get saved.

It seemed like God really wanted him to be in active ministry, and Sam really wanted to be, but the invitations to preach were few and far between, and lots of doors slammed in his face. He wasn't getting enough meetings to make ends meet, so he couldn't quit his day job.

He was frustrated. He knew that God had called him to be an evangelist, and the fruit was there, but nothing else seemed to be happening.

One day Sam went to church and heard his pastor preach a message about forgiveness. At the end of the service, the Lord spoke to Sam's heart and said, "You need to forgive your father."

"You need to forgive your father."

Here's a little bit of the back story: Sam's parents had split up when he was just a youngster, and when his dad remarried right away, he and his new wife had several children. As a result, as so often happens, most of Sam's dad's resources and attention went to the new family. That left Sam and his mom and sister to deal with all the economic and emotional ramifications of being the family left behind.

Now, Sam had forgiven his father before, numerous times. But how many of us have forgiven someone once (or twice or many times) only to find that the thoughts and feelings sometimes sneak back in? And pretty soon we find ourselves in unforgiveness land again, holding a grudge and frowning every time their name comes up.

Sometimes the transgressions of the person we've forgiven go on and on, and need to be *constantly* forgiven. (We talked about forgiving again and again in chapter 2.)

That's where Sam found himself. He didn't even realize that he'd begun feeling bad again about his dad until the Lord pointed it out to him. Thank God for his Word, and faithful ministers to preach it to us when we need a reminder.

Free to Fulfill His Calling

The good news is that it didn't take Sam long to forgive again once he realized he needed to. He simply prayed, "Father, forgive me, I didn't know I was back in unforgiveness! Thank you for revealing it to me. I lift up my dad to you again, and I forgive him for everything, in Jesus' Name. Thank you Lord, amen."

Immediately a peace and joy filled Sam's heart, and he knew he was right on in obedience to God. He literally felt free.

But the story doesn't end there! Amazingly enough, within a week of forgiving his dad again, Sam began to get calls requesting him to come and minister. His schedule began to fill up with ministry opportunities, and I'm happy to say that today, he is in full-time traveling evangelistic ministry.

True For All of Us

While the stories in this chapter are about ministers and apply directly to life in ministry, the same truths apply to all of us. It always pays to forgive. We don't want the trap of unforgiveness to steal any of God's blessings in our lives – his peace, his calling, his healing – anything! God has so many wonderful things in store for us, and when he prompts us to forgive, it's so that we can continue to walk in all his blessings.

Questions for Reflection and Discussion >>

• Can you identify with Pastor Hank? Have you ever felt unappreciated? What happened?

• Is there anyone you have had trouble forgiving after you've poured your life out for them?

• What does "living for an audience of One" mean to you?

Chapter 7

Forgiving Yourself

Right here we're going to digress a bit from the title of this book and shift from forgiving others to forgiving that hardest person of all. Yourself. Instead of the title "I Forgive You, But . . . ." for this chapter we could say it this way: "I Know God Forgives Me, But . . . ."

Because everywhere I go, I meet people who feel like they can't forgive themselves. And I get it. I think the hardest person to forgive is yourself. We humans often tend to be harder on ourselves than anyone else. Maybe you can easily forgive others, but can find no justification for forgiving yourself.

Everywhere I go, I meet people who feel like they can't forgive themselves.

Maybe you won't even consider forgiving yourself because you feel like you have to keep yourself in a state of constant remembrance so you don't forget. Or maybe you believe there is some sort of lifelong penance you must pay because you've seen your failure up close and personal, and you've lived with it. You might have even known better, but you goofed up big time anyway. And now you've listened to the accuser of the brethren (Satan) enough to know what you deserve as a result.

But, as we've seen through the previous chapters, forgiveness is vital to living a life of peace, freedom, and power. And that includes forgiving yourself. It's just as important as forgiving others.

I have a friend who had an abortion years ago when she was young. There are few things harder to forgive than taking the life of a precious innocent baby, so I asked her to share the process she went through to receive forgiveness in her own life.

Cut to the Heart

Kim's Story: "Many years ago, I heard a message preached on the subject of forgiveness. My husband and I had traveled to a city several hours away from our hometown to hear this speaker, Rev. Roy Hicks, and he preached a cut-to-the-heart type of message. Although I can't remember the details now, at the time it profoundly stuck to me, like glue.

"After the service, as we began our journey home, I was laying in the back of our van and thought over all I had heard that day. I knew that if I didn't forgive others I would also not be forgiven. This was alarming to me, so I began to search my heart.

"At this point I thought I had moved on from past wounds and tried to bury them. Yet, as I lay quietly in the back of the van, I knew one person that I had never gone through the process of forgiving. It was my first husband. He was four years older than I was when we were dating, and he was very persuasive. He had manipulated me to have sex when I was just a teenager.

"As a result, at 18 I became pregnant. We planned to wed right after I graduated from high school, and he convinced me to keep my pregnancy a secret. He promised me a bright future, and although I was scared, I was excited to be a mommy.

"But right after the wedding came a crushing blow. He began to bombard me about aborting my child. I was horrified at first and refused to even talk about it. But day after day, week after week, month after month he continued to wear me down. So I finally agreed to at least go see a doctor, but I still didn't plan to abort the baby.

"Unfortunately, that quickly progressed into plans to have an abortion. Although I didn't want to, I was swayed through much imploring on my spouse's part, and I finally agreed. I had no idea what I was doing, nor did I realize the pain, shame and heartache I would have to live with for the next 30 years."

Forgive Yourself

"That horrible memory is what was playing through my mind that day in the back of the van as we drove home. I realized I needed to forgive my first husband. Our marriage had only lasted 3 ½ years and I was now happily remarried.

"I quietly and truthfully repented and let go of all animosity and anguish from the brokenness of this past painful relationship. As I lay quietly I heard the soft sweet voice of the Lord in my heart. He said, 'Now, you need to forgive yourself.'

The Lord's voice was so soft and quiet. Outside I heard the sound of the van engine and the tires on the freeway, yet inside my heart his words were very distinctive. Then from the stillness of my heart, his whisper within came again. 'Forgive yourself,' He said.

"I lay still with tears streaming down my face as I contemplated what I had heard. Forgive yourself. I heard it twice. Sobbing quietly, I forgave myself for the horrendous and unconscionable deed I had allowed to happen to my body and my child.

"I will always regret what happened, and if I could turn back the clock I would. But I had to move forward. After forgiving my first husband and myself in that back of that van, I was able to put it behind me once and for all. It was a process of one step after another, but it was so good to be in a place of freedom and not under the bondage of unforgiveness any longer.

"Forgiving ourselves is a part of God's plan to keep us free."

"Often, I think we don't realize that forgiving ourselves is a part of God's plan to keep us free. That was a momentous event in my life. I could definitely tell a difference after I prayed in the back of that van, and I've never forgotten the moment I forgave myself and got free."

Destined to Pay Forever?

The devil would love to keep you in bondage to your past sins. Legally, he doesn't have a leg to stand on, but if he can get you to keep thinking about what you've done — feeling guilty and unworthy in the face of your trespass — then he's got you right where he wants you. You aren't going to be praying any great faith prayers, or walking out God's plan for your life, or helping anyone else when you're playing your guilt and your sin on a loop in your head day after day.

You might be embarrassed, humiliated, or disgusted by what you've done (or haven't done), and maybe you have a healthy dose of fear thrown into the mix — fear of people finding out, fear of being ostracized by your church or by people who matter to you. Maybe you're drowning in shame because someone already has found out.

Well, I have news for you. No one is perfect. Every single person you know has blown it at one time or another — big time. So where does that leave you? Are you stuck here, destined to pay for your mistake forever?

I meet a lot of people who are living by that old saying, "You made this bed, now you have to lie in it." But I can't find that in the Bible anywhere! Nowhere does it say, "Too bad you made that wrong decision — now you're disqualified; it's over for you."

In fact, I read in Romans 8:1 that there is no condemnation to those who are in Christ Jesus and in Ephesians 2:4 that he is rich in mercy and loves you greatly!

God Has Forgiven You

If you are a Christian, then God has forgiven you. It's that simple. You can't earn or deserve this forgiveness. You received it when you received Christ as your Savior. (If you haven't done that yet but you want to, go to page ___, pray the prayer, and come back to keep reading). Your forgiveness is already a done deal, not based on what you've done or haven't done, but based on what Jesus did for you.

Second Corinthians 5:19 says, "It was God [personally present] in Christ, reconciling and restoring the world to favor with Himself, not counting up and holding against [men] their trespasses [but cancelling them], and committing to us the message of reconciliation (of the restoration to favor)" (AMPC). God is not mad at you. He's already forgiven. It's up to us to believe that and accept the restored relationship he's offering.

There is never again a reason to be estranged from God or go without his help and blessing because you can't forgive yourself. First John 2:12 says, "I write to you, little children, because your sins are forgiven you for his name's sake."

No matter what you have done, God's already forgiven you for his Name's sake. And he loves you. You can rest assured that forgiving you was God's idea. Now it's up to you to believe that he's already done it, thank him for it, and forgive yourself. Jesus Christ already paid the price for all of your sins, and God is no longer holding any sin against you! You have been forgiven.

How Far Is East from West?

Psalm 103:12 says, "As far as the east is from the west, so far has he removed our transgressions from us."

God isn't keeping track of your mistakes and transgressions, so you shouldn't either. Think about that verse for a minute. On this planet, we do have a measurement of how far the north is from the south. When I was looking up this fact, I found all sorts of answers to "how far is the north pole from the south pole" because it depends on how you measure it. For example, straight through the earth from pole to pole it's 7,899 miles; if you go halfway around the planet from pole to pole it's 12,429 miles. But the point is, there is a north point and a south point to measure from, so there is a way of telling how far the north is from the south.

But where is east? And where is west? There are no points to measure from, so there's no way of knowing how far the east is from the west! And that's exactly God's point. He's not measuring. He has made sure there's no way of keeping track of your transgressions. They're gone.

So from God's point of view, there's never anything standing between you and him. No one does forgiveness better than God. Isaiah 1:18 says, "Though your sins are like scarlet, they shall be as white as snow; though they are red like crimson, they shall be as wool." If you've been unable to forgive yourself, it's time for you to start seeing yourself as God does — white as snow. Without sin. Blameless and pure in God's sight.

....

If you've been unable to forgive yourself, it's time for you to start seeing yourself as God does.

....

I love what God says in Hebrews 10:16–17. It's a quote from Jeremiah 31:33–34, talking about the covenant he was planning to make with mankind (you and me) through Jesus. He says, "This is the covenant that I will make with them after those days, says the Lord: I will put My laws into their hearts, and in their minds I will write them . . . their sins and their lawless deeds I will remember no more."

This is the covenant you and I are walking in today if we have accepted Jesus as our Savior. God wrote his law right on our hearts and in our minds, not on tablets. He's that close to us. He made us into new creatures, to be just like him. And he simply will not remember or keep track of our sins and trespasses.

Isn't that good news? It's time we believe that, and live like it's true. If God says he will remember your sin and lawless deeds no more, he means it. Instead of letting guilt and shame dominate your thoughts, you can do like this verse says and let his law and his love dominate your mind.

How to Move Forward

So what should you do if you've blown it? Ask God to forgive you. The Bible says, "If we confess our sins, He is faithful and just to forgive us our sins and to cleanse us from all unrighteousness" (1 John 1:9). God knew you would goof up — he knew all of us would — so he made provision for it.

As a Christian, you are already righteous in God's sight through Jesus Christ (2 Cor. 5:21). So what is this verse talking about? It's talking about another chance. It's not talking about your sin *condition* — that's already been paid for by the blood of Jesus, and now you're a new creature with his nature inside of you. This is talking about when you transgress (commit transgressions) and need forgiveness instead of guilt, mercy instead of judgement.

I love this verse, because it shows us exactly what to do when we've goofed up (and we all have). It says first, tell God about it (confess your sins). Now trust me when I tell you: when you confess is not the first time he's heard about. He already knows you goofed up! The confession is for *you*.

Just like in the Garden of Eden, when Adam and Eve sinned and God showed up, asking them "What have you done?" (Gen. 3:13). Do you think God really didn't know what they'd done? Of course he knew. He asked so they would know, and acknowledge their wrongdoing. As always, he's more interested in our heart and our character than anything else.

Then the next part of that verse in 1 John is my favorite: after you confess, "He is faithful and just to forgive." Is he faithful? Yes! He is faithful even when we are not (2 Tim. 2:13). This forgiveness you're asking for isn't based on you and what you've done, it's based on his faithfulness. Oh thank God!

This forgiveness you're asking for isn't based on you and what you've done, it's based on his faithfulness.

So if you've goofed up, it's time to forgive yourself. Pray this: "Heavenly Father, I confess that I sinned (tell him what it is). Please forgive me and cleanse me from the propensity to sin again. Thank you for your faithfulness! I receive your forgiveness, in Jesus Name, amen."

Good Company

There are those who might say it's not that simple, especially if there are other people involved. Granted, your failure or bad choice may have set off a chain of events that can't be reversed, and maybe there are a lot of lives, yours included, that are affected very badly as a result of what you've done.

But here's the deal. You can't rewrite the past. Beating yourself up over it isn't going to change anything, and it's going to hinder you (and probably others) from moving forward. It's also going to make you (and everyone around you) miserable. Maybe an apology or some kind of restitution is required (ask God), but refusing to forgive yourself is not the right answer.

I want you to know that whatever you've done, you're in good company. The Bible has many, many examples of people who goofed up big time, but God forgave them, and still used them. They still fulfilled their divine destiny. You may have seen this list before:

• Noah was a drunk.

• Jacob was a liar.

• Moses was a murderer.

- Samson was a womanizer.
- Rahab was a prostitute.
- David was an adulterer (not to mention a murderer).
- Jonah ran from God.
- Job went bankrupt.
- Peter denied Christ.
- All the disciples fell asleep while praying (and ran away when Jesus really needed them).
- Martha worried about everything.
- The Samaritan woman was divorced (more than once).
- Mary Magdalene was demon-possessed.
- Paul was a Christian-killer.

God has only had humans to work with for his entire career. He is not freaked out over you. No matter what condemnation the devil has been whispering in your ear, he is a liar and wants to render you useless to the kingdom of God. Every saint has a past and every sinner has a future. Nobody can go back and make a new beginning, but anyone can start today and make a new ending.

Every saint has a past, and every sinner has a future.

Forgiving yourself isn't about letting yourself off the hook, or justifying what you've done. It's about believing what God has said about you in his Word. It's a choice that takes courage and strength, and it gives you the opportunity to become an overcomer rather than remaining a victim of your own scorn.

Forget and Press Forward

The apostle Paul knew about the courage to forget and move on. He said it this way, "One thing I do, forgetting those things which are behind and reaching forward to those things which are ahead, I press toward the goal for the prize of the upward call of God in Christ Jesus" (Phil. 3:13–14).

Now, Paul had some pretty major things behind him to forget. He made a lot more wrong decisions than you have. For one thing, he had a part in murdering Christians! My guess is that you haven't missed it that badly.

So this verse applies to you and your situation. You *can* move on from blowing it. Don't beat yourself up over it. Be like Paul and put it behind you.

> *You can move on from blowing it.*
> *Be like Paul and put it behind you.*

Yes, it's better to never goof up, but we humans are far from perfect. *Everyone* has made mistakes and wrong decisions. It doesn't matter how many times you fall down; all that matters is how many times you get back up again.

One of my favorite verses in the Bible is Micah 7:8: "Do not rejoice over me, my enemy; When I fall, I will arise." Everyone is going to trip up or fall down. That's why this verse is in the Bible. God knows exactly how we humans are. But here he's saying that all you have to do is get up one more time than you fall down! You're only defeated when you give up.

It might take a while, but you can count on God. He knows exactly how to help you get back on track and put things back together, even if other people were involved. He is the God of the second chance. In fact, I once heard someone say he is the God of *another* chance. That's good news, because sometimes we even mess up the second chance!

God is incredibly patient with us. He is full of grace and mercy. He doesn't disqualify us when we blow it. Psalm 86:15 says, "But you, O Lord, are a God of compassion and mercy, slow to get angry and filled with unfailing love and faithfulness" (NLT). Micah 7:18 says, "Who is a God like You, pardoning iniquity and passing over the transgression of the remnant of his heritage? He does not retain his anger forever, because he delights in mercy."

I want to encourage you today, if you've blown it, get up and go again. Forgive yourself and move on. Put the past behind you and trust God to help you put things back together. He knows just how to do it.

When You Keep Doing It

Maybe you've asked for forgiveness over and over again, but you keep falling back into sin. It's one thing to forgive yourself once, but it seems almost impossible to forgive yourself

---

It's one thing to forgive yourself once,
but it seems almost impossible to forgive yourself again
and again for the same thing.

Gary's Story: I knew a young man — let's call him Gary — who had a drinking problem. After he got saved, he would remain sober for a while, but then every time life's pressures came, he would fall back into drinking. It was his fallback coping mechanism. As a result, Gary was filled with self-loathing.

"Everything would go along fine for a while," he said, "but then something would happen, and I would drink again. It was like going down a road just fine, but then the road drops off a cliff. I could see the cliff coming, but like a fool I just kept walking toward it.

"I wanted to quit completely, I prayed to quit completely, I *tried* to quit, but I just kept falling off the cliff. I felt like I was letting the Lord down, which I hated. And besides, I didn't have time to mess with drinking. I had a business to run and people to take care of. My father was an alcoholic, and I knew what the Bible said about the sins of the fathers being passed down to the next generation."

Gary was mired in guilt and felt as if God couldn't forgive him over and over. The devil loves it when that happens, because it makes us want to give up. Satan was trying to hold Gary in bondage to guilt and sin, even using Old Testament scripture to condemn him.

But the truth is, as a new creature in Christ (2 Cor. 5:17), Gary was redeemed from his father's bloodline. Ephesians 1:7 says that in Jesus, "we have redemption through his blood, the forgiveness of sins," and Hebrews 9:28 says that the blood of "Christ was offered once to bear the sins of many."

Thankfully, two great things happened in Gary's life. First, he went to a recovery group to get the help he needed, and second, he began to meditate on what the Bible says, and he believed it.

"I found out that God is merciful," he says. "He sent Jesus to bear my sins and set me free. From meditating on the Word, I realized that I'm not bound by the sins of my father anymore. I come from a new bloodline now. I was able to forgive myself when I realized Romans 6 belonged to me."

Here are just a few of the verses from Romans 6 that helped Gary to forgive himself and live free:

> Now if we died with Christ, we believe that we shall also live with Him, [9] knowing that Christ, having been raised from the dead, dies no more. Death no longer has dominion over Him. [10] For the death that He died, He died to sin once for all; but the life that He lives, He lives to God. [11] Likewise you also, reckon yourselves to be dead indeed to sin, but alive to God in Christ Jesus our Lord. [12] Therefore do not let sin reign in your mortal body, that you should obey it in its lusts. [13] And do not present your members as instruments of unrighteousness to sin, but present yourselves to God as being alive from the dead, and your members as instruments of righteousness to God. [14] For sin shall not have dominion over you, for you are not under law but under grace.
>
> vv. 8–14

When we reckon ourselves to be dead to sin, it has no more dominion over us! That's just as true for you as it was for Gary. As he got this truth down into his spirit, he was able to "present himself to God as being alive from the dead" and sin had no more dominion over him. In Jesus, there is always hope, always another chance.

Change Your Mind

Just as we talked about in chapter 2, the key to forgiving is in your head: your thoughts. The same is true with forgiving yourself. If you keep letting the devil rehearse your mistakes and failures, and you keep meditating on what you "deserve" because of it, you're going to be defeated.

The key to freedom and receiving true forgiveness is in changing — or renewing — your mind to what God says about you. Because, as we've seen, God isn't keeping track of your sin or making you pay for them. Jesus already paid.

Your righteousness and acceptance as a Christian isn't based on your actions; it's based on your covenant through Christ. Ephesians 1:6 says you are "accepted in the beloved" not because of what you've done (by earning or deserving), but because of what Jesus did (1 Pet. 2:24). It's already done.

Your righteousness isn't based on your actions; it's based on your covenant.

The key to walking in this forgiveness is, simply put, to think about it. Change your thoughts from what the devil has been telling you (condemnation and shame, rehearsing your failure and what you deserve as a result) to what God is telling you (you're righteous, beloved, and forgiven in Christ).

You change your thoughts by *meditating* (thinking on) the Word of God. Replacing thoughts of condemnation and shame with what God says about you. That's what step 2 in this book is for — reading and speaking God's Word over your life.

Questions for Reflection and Discussion >>

- Do you have trouble forgiving yourself? Why or why not?
- Have you ever felt like "you made this bed, and now you have to lie in it?" Do you still feel that way after reading this chapter?
- Does forgiving yourself feel possible to you now?
- Why is it important to forgive yourself?

·············· **Chapter 8** ··············

So Many Opportunities to Forgive!

When you picked up this book, you may have had a specific event or person in mind that needed forgiving. Some of us have had very painful things happen to us — even a long time ago — that need to be forgiven. I trust this book has been a help to you in doing that, so you can have the peace in your life that God has promised.

But aside from being able to forgive and put those major issues behind us, I'm hoping that we can all get a little bit better at living a *lifestyle* of forgiveness. You know, where nothing bothers us, where small (and even large) offenses can just roll off us like water off a duck's back. I think that sounds like a life of peace, don't you?

···

I'm hoping we can all get a little bit better at living a lifestyle of forgiveness.

···

It's the Little Things

So many things happen to us in a day, and it seems like there are just a lot of opportunities to be irritated, get mad, get even, or hold a grudge. The Bible says it's the little foxes that spoil the vine (Song 2:15). It's not always the big things, but the little annoyances that get us reacting in the flesh, stealing our peace, and possibly clogging our blessing pipe.

We live in a society that is quick to blame, quick to get angry or feel put upon, and quick to vent when things don't go our way. If you think about it, that's really the opposite of the way God wants us to live.

My Story: One day I had to take my husband's car to the dealership for a repair. After it was all done, I headed for the payment counter to settle the bill. One of the dealership employees was at the desk before me, talking about something with the woman behind the counter.

When she left and I stepped up to take my turn, I almost laughed out loud at the expression on the face of the woman behind the counter. Her face was all puckered up and her eyebrows were furrowed in an angry glare. She looked like she had just sucked on a lemon!

"Hi," I said as I presented my paperwork to her. In response she swiped at her face and began making little "puff" noises with her nose and mouth, as if she was trying to rid herself of a pesky bug.

So I asked her, "Are you okay?"

With an expression of deep offense, she nodded in the direction of her departed fellow-employee and said haughtily, "Her perfume is just so strong! I like some smells, but her perfume really gets to me." Everything about her tone and demeanor was saying, "How dare she wear that perfume?"

I managed to keep from laughing out loud at the poor woman, but I thought to myself, "It's so easy to become offended, isn't it? Even over small stuff!" I doubt that her fellow employee wore the perfume on purpose just to bug her. I was sorry it affected her so badly, but I wondered if she would let this event color her whole day.

Sometimes that happens, doesn't it? Intentionally or unintentionally, someone ticks us off, even in a minor way, and we let it get under our skin and bug us all day long.

But what if we got so good at quickly and easily forgiving that instead of notifying everyone that we're ticked off, we didn't even notice those things?

....

What if we got so good at forgiving that instead
of notifying everyone that we're ticked off,
we didn't even notice?

....

What if we really *acted on* 1 Corinthians 13:5, which says that love "does not behave rudely, does not seek its own, is not provoked, thinks no evil?" The Classic Amplified Bible says, "*it takes no account of the evil done to it [it pays no attention to a suffered wrong].*"

Wow, is that even possible? Can you imagine, when someone does something that hurts you or makes you mad, that you would take no notice of it, *pay no attention* to it? If, when someone offends you (intentionally or not), you just forgive automatically, before offense *even has a chance to hit your heart or get stuck in your mind?

I think it's in the Bible for a reason. Yes, I think it's possible! I think it's life of freedom! And we can do it because God's love resides in us. Romans 5:5 says, "The love of God has been poured out in our hearts by the Holy Spirit who was given to us." God's agape, unconditional love is in us! Not natural human love — not an ooey-gooey feeling — but the supernatural God-kind of love is already in the heart of every believer. That means you and I can make a choice every day to yield to it.

Living that way every day will take some practice, for sure. But we can't even begin that journey unless we're aware of it and we want to act on it.

I think the only way to walk in this kind of love is to get really good at forgiving the big things *and* the small things. The better we get at forgiving the little irritations and "unfairnesses" of life on a day-to-day basis, the easier it is for us to forgive truly painful events in our lives.

The only way to walk in this kind of love is to get really good at forgiving

How do we get better at something? We have to practice. To get better at playing the piano, we have to practice. To get better at giving speeches, we have to do it more. To get better at playing any kind of sport, we have to practice.

I think it's the same with forgiveness. The more we practice, the better we get at it. And if we practice forgiving the small things — the little daily irritations — then I'm pretty sure that we're more ready to forgive when big hurts come along. Then we can walk away from the hurt with barely a scratch on us. Which means we can live in freedom and keep our blessing pipe flowing *all the time*. I believe that's how God wants us to live, and he's empowered us to do it.

A Sample List

Here are just a few of the everyday adventures that happen to all of us — things that may drive us nuts, but that we might consider forgiving instantly.

• **Drivers in the left lane.** Okay, this is my own personal pet peeve. I live in a city, and most of the time there are two lanes for traffic. *Why* do the slow drivers insist on clogging up the left lane? I'm in a hurry here, people! Yet I have a choice. I can drive behind them, impatient and irritated, talking to them and about them ("Hey buddy, are you the only one on the road? Are you paying any attention at all? Move over!"), or I can bless and forgive them. Because really, does my impatience do any good? Or does it just make my blood pressure go up and feed my habit of unforgiveness? (Ouch). Variations of this pet peeve include drivers in general (turning without using blinkers, driving with a blinker permanently *on*, tailgaters, those who can't read signs, etc.) or slow people walking five abreast in an airport concourse so *no one* else can get by (not that it's ever happened to me, of course). Forgive them, Lord. Bless them.

- **Neighbors.** There are endless things a neighbor can do to tick you off. Loud dogs. Loud music. Loud shouting. Any and *all* forms of loud. Annoying vehicles. Messy yard. Bright lights that shine in the window when you're trying to sleep. Setting off fireworks endlessly before and after July 4 (and New Year's!). Letting their dog poop in your yard. Leaving their garbage cans out. Parking where they shouldn't. Complaining about *you* being too loud, or letting your dog run loose, or not mowing your yard, or setting off firecrackers, or parking where you shouldn't. You get the picture. Have you been mad about it? How's that been working for you? Did it change their behavior in any way? I'm guessing no. Maybe forgiving would work better (and be a better witness) and allow God to move in the situation. Matthew 19:19 says, "You shall love your neighbor as yourself." It doesn't say "if they deserve it."

- **Those in your household.** The people we're around the most are the ones who have the most potential to irritate us, offend us, or hurt our feelings. For one thing, we spend a lot of time with them. For another, we expect more out of them. But people will always disappoint and irritate us (even loved ones), just as we disappoint and irritate them. Rather than holding onto those irritations (or using them as weapons in the next argument), what if we aimed for peace in our household and just got good at forgiving quickly and easily? James 3:17 says, "Real wisdom, God's wisdom, begins with a holy life and *is characterized by getting along with others*. It is gentle and reasonable, overflowing with mercy and blessings, not hot one day and cold the next" (MSG, emphasis mine).

- **Family in general.** I'm writing this book at holiday time, and I had an interesting chat with a friend the other day about getting together with family, as so many of us do at holiday time. There is an older person in her family who is very grumpy, picky, and critical. The way my friend described it was this person "takes the whole family hostage," meaning they don't want to do this or that, they won't eat this or that, things have to be done a certain way, everyone does it wrong, and so on. I could tell it was very stressful for my friend. There can be many variations on this theme, but very often one (or more) person can change the dynamics in a family. I fully believe in laying down some healthy, rational boundaries for people like that (even relatives). But *forgive* first, to be sure your heart is right. I believe that forgiving them (often if necessary!) rather than talking about them or dreading their presence, makes it possible for God to move in their lives. Not to mention that forgiving will help you keep your peace and your blessing pipe clear! Romans 14:19 says: "Therefore let us pursue the things which make for peace and the things by which one may edify another."

- **Being slighted.** It's so easy to get offended (and hold a grudge) when someone slights us or doesn't give us our due. Maybe you waved at someone and they didn't wave back. Maybe someone said something with the wrong tone or facial expression, or maybe they talked down to you or made you feel stupid in a group. Or maybe someone didn't answer your text or phone call, and you start *imagining* all the reasons why: "Maybe she's mad, or she hates me, or she's a snob! That's it, I'm never speaking to her again!" when in reality there could be a perfectly good reason. Rather than taking things personally or being hurt or angry over being slighted or made to feel stupid, might I suggest forgiving instead? Proverbs 12:16 says, "Fools have short fuses and explode all too quickly; the prudent quietly shrug off insults" (MSG). Forgiveness lets you walk away and forget it (shrug it off), not letting the pain or irritation stick to you.

- **Violated expectancies.** We all have expectancies, every single day. We expect people to act a certain way. We expect things to go a certain way. We expect to be understood or revered. But the chances of everything happening exactly the way we expect it to is — brace yourself — ZERO. Every single day, in a hundred different scenarios, your expectancies will be violated. We could talk about each and every way that could happen, but that's another book. For now, I'm trusting the Holy Spirit to bring this to your remembrance when you need it and help you realize when your expectancies have been violated, and help you forgive quickly and easily when it happens.

The list could go on and on. Someone cutting you off in traffic, cutting in line at the store, or grabbing the last one of an item that you really wanted. Anytime you get the "rot gut" feeling, where you're embarrassed, sad, angry, rejected, or hurt, those are the times to ask yourself, "Is there anyone I need to forgive, so I can walk away free?"

And let me just add this: Sometimes you know that someone didn't mean to hurt you, and you recognize that you're being sort of ridiculous over something insignificant. You might think, "I don't need to forgive them. It's not even a big deal. I know I'm being weird about it." Here's my rule: if you thought about it more than twice, just go ahead and forgive them!

If you thought about it more than twice, just go ahead and forgive them!

When that guy posts something ridiculous on social media and you're so bugged about it that you want to tell everyone when you get to work, just go ahead and forgive him. When that lady at the store is so rude to you that you have an imaginary conversation in your head all the way home ("I should've said *this*, and when she said *that*, I would've said *this*!"), just go ahead and forgive her.

I believe if we get good at forgiving people in the relatively minor, everyday things, we'll be in good practice for the truly big things. Plus, we'll live a life of peace and be a good witness.

How I Got Off the Self-Pity Train

You might wonder what self-pity has to do with forgiveness, but here's what I've learned: when I feel sorry for myself, sometimes it's because someone has said something or done something that violated my expectancies or hurt my feelings. So whenever I get that "poor me" feeling, I've learned that the first thing I do is ask myself, "Is there anyone I need to forgive?"

Because I can't have faith and feel sorry for myself at the same time. When somebody hurts me, irritates me, or does me wrong, it's *so easy* to feel like a victim. Poor me! How dare they?

> *I can't have faith and feel sorry for myself at the same time.*

And as soon as those thoughts go round in my head a few times, inevitably I become completely consumed with my own world and what's happening in it. I become the center of my own attention, the star of my own misery show, and I cease to think of anyone but myself. When I start having a self-pity party, I've elevated my own importance in my own eyes , and Romans 12:3 says, "For I say, through the grace given to me, to everyone who is among you, not to think of himself more highly than he ought to think."

The moment I let life's hurts and injustices dictate my emotions, I'm thinking too highly of myself. Self-pity can lead to bitterness, and that can quickly override the fruit of the Spirit which should be dominating my life.

First Thessalonians 5:18 tells us not to "quench the Holy Spirit," but instead give thanks in everything. You and I both know that it's hard to give thanks in the middle of a self-pity party! A self-indulgent attitude isn't focused on gratitude, is it?

When I'm thinking only of myself and my "poor me" circumstances, you could say that I have a one-way ticket on the self-pity train, and it's zooming along at breakneck speed!

Well, I was on that train one day after someone had hurt my feelings, and I happened to be reading in 2 Corinthians 4. When I got to verses 17 and 18 I read: "For our light affliction, which is but for a moment, is working for us a far more exceeding and eternal weight of glory, while we do not look at the things which are seen, but at the things which are not seen. For the things which are seen are temporary, but the things which are not seen are eternal."

Right at that moment, I felt like the Lord spoke to my heart, saying, "If you want this 'affliction' to be light and temporary, don't focus on what you see or feel — focus on my truths!" Instantly, I could see what he was saying. Feeling sorry for myself kept me from forgiving the person who hurt me and kept my focus on myself and the pain I was feeling. If I wanted to be free, I needed to focus on something else — on God's goodness!

I realized that yes, I might have been hurt, I might have a mess to deal with, a struggle to overcome, a story to tell, but I didn't want to stay there. Almost all of us have been hurt or betrayed at some point in our life.

It made me stop, reevaluate, and decide to stop the self-pity train right there. Yes, life can be painful and messy, but I am not going to let those moments define me. I'm going to rise up and put it behind me. The fastest way I've found to do that is to forgive and simply let it go.

I decided that I'm not some fragile creature who needs to be watched and worried over. I'm a grown-up, and I can be resilient when stuff gets thrown at me. I'm the one who forgives, quickly and easily! I'm going to get into the Word, put my shoulders back, keep my head up and determine to put the past behind and move forward.

Want to join me?

Questions for Reflection and Discussion >>

• What's the problem with letting the little things bother you?

• Do you think it's possible to follow 1 Corinthians 13:5 and "take no notice of or *pay no attention* to" when someone does you wrong?

• What does it mean to be on the self-pity train? What do you think about it now?

• What stood out to you most in this chapter?

STEP 2

Meditate and Declare This

Hurray, you made it through step 1. Good job! I hope you're feeling encouraged. Step 2 is all of the scriptures we've talked about in the first step. They're all written down, with declarations, making it easy for you to meditate and declare them for your own life.

Read these scriptures each day for as long as you need to. Speak them aloud and think on them. Mark the ones that mean the most to you: highlight them, put stars by them, add a sticky note. When hurt feelings come up, come back to read and speak them again. Once is not enough! This is how we replace the painful thoughts with God's thoughts. This is how we get free. Bathe your spirit in this Word, and return here as often as needed.

·············· From Chapter 1 ··············

Life Is So Unfair

Read and think about it: When you were dead in your transgressions and the uncircumcision of your flesh, He made you alive together with Him, having forgiven us all our transgressions (Col. 2:13 NASB).

Declare: Forgiveness is how my relationship started with God. It's how he made me a new creature, alive together with him. Forgiveness is how God starts fresh — how he does do-overs. I want to start fresh and forgive.

·························

Read and think about it: I, even I, am He who blots out your transgressions for My own sake; and I will not remember your sins (Is. 43:25).

Declare: God's way of dealing with mankind is forgiveness. He never has unforgiveness in his relationship with me – he never remembers my sins. I have God's very nature inside me, so I've not only been forgiven, but I have the capacity to forgive. I choose God's way – I forgive.

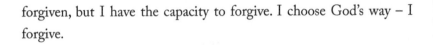

Read and think about it: I call heaven and earth as witnesses today against you, that I have set before you life and death, blessing and cursing; therefore choose life, that both you and your descendants may live (Deut. 30:19).

Declare: God is not going to make me forgive. It's my choice. So I choose to forgive, and because I do, I know he's standing by, ready to help me do it. Forgiveness is my best option. It's the path to freedom.

Read and think about it: Be kind to one another, tenderhearted, forgiving one another, just as God in Christ also forgave you (Eph. 4:32).

Declare: I realize that if I don't choose to deal with people in the same manner God does (by forgiving), then I'm disobeying his commandment and I'm outside of his domain, so I can expect the result of that in my life. I know I can't go against his nature (by harboring unforgiveness) and expect his blessings to flow to me. So I will forgive. I won't clog my blessing pipe.

Read and think about it: God is light and in Him is no darkness at all. . . . Every good gift and every perfect gift is from above, and comes down from the Father of lights, with whom there is no variation or shadow of turning (1 John 1:5, James 1:17).

Declare: When I wonder how God could let something happen, why he didn't stop it, or why he didn't answer my prayer the way I thought he should, I'll remember that God is not my enemy. All of his intentions and actions toward me are good, not bad. He doesn't change back and forth from good to bad, sometimes blessing and sometimes cursing. So I don't hold any anger or malice in my heart toward him. I trust him.

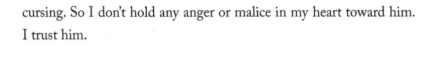

Read and think about it: The thief does not come except to steal, and to kill, and to destroy. I have come that they may have life, and that they may have it more abundantly (John 10:10).

Declare: I'm not confused about who causes what in my life. If there's any stealing, killing, or destroying going on, it's from the devil, not God! God is a good and loving Father, who wants only the best for me. He has given me abundant life in Jesus.

Read and think about it: For we do not wrestle against flesh and blood, but against principalities, against powers, against the rulers of the darkness of this age, against spiritual hosts of wickedness in the heavenly places (Eph. 6:12).

Declare: I will remember that people are not my enemy. Satan will sow seeds of division, strife and unforgiveness into my life because he wants me to live and react in the lower realm of the flesh to stop God's blessings from flowing to me. I won't allow it by "wrestling" with people. Instead I recognize where that spirit of strife, division, and offense is coming from, and I take authority over the devil, in Jesus Name!

Read and think about it: Now whom you forgive anything, I also forgive…lest Satan should take advantage of us; for we are not ignorant of his devices (2 Cor. 1:10–11).

Declare: When I feel hurt or angry at someone, or things are going wrong in my life, I will stop and remember that it's coming from the devil. So I won't focus on hurts and disappointments; instead, I'll remember who I am in Christ, why I'm here, and what I'm called to. I'm not ignorant of his devices! I'll turn the tables on him by forgiving.

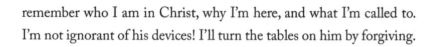

Read and think about it: But love your enemies, do good, and lend, hoping for nothing in return; and your reward will be great, and you will be sons of the Most High. For He is kind to the unthankful and evil. Therefore be merciful, just as your Father also is merciful. Judge not, and you shall not be judged. Condemn not, and you shall not be condemned. Forgive, and you will be forgiven (Luke 6:35–37).

Declare: I will love my enemies, do good, lend and look for nothing in return, be merciful, not judge, not condemn, and forgive. These are God's instructions for life, and I'm willing to live by them, knowing that he's helping me do it. He's not asking me to try to be perfect; he's asking me to let him live through me. I can do that!

Read and think about it: But God demonstrates his own love toward us, in that while we were still sinners, Christ died for us (Rom. 5:8).

Declare: God forgave me when I didn't deserve it. So I can forgive people when they don't deserve it. God forgave me in Jesus because he's good, not because I'm good. He didn't view forgiveness as an option, but as a covenant. It's not based on how I behave, but on his determination to love at all costs.

Read and think about it: Even as Christ forgave you, so you also must do (Col. 3:13).

Declare: Christ forgave me without strings attached, out of his great mercy and love. Since he did, I must forgive too. It's not an option, it's a commandment. And I know that when I obey the Lord's

142

commandments, things go well with me. Loving God means keeping his commandments, and it's not hard (1 John 5:3).

Read and think about it: Let us lay aside every weight, and the sin which so easily ensnares us, and let us run with endurance the race that is set before us (Heb. 12:1).

Declare: Holding onto unforgiveness is like attaching a ball and chain to my ankle; then every time I try to run my race it bangs against my leg, hindering my progress and causing me pain. It's bondage! When I forgive it's laying aside that weight — it's cutting that chain so I can run unhindered into my future with peace and freedom.

Read and think about it: And whenever you stand praying, if you have anything against anyone, forgive him and let it drop (leave it, let it go), in order that your Father Who is in heaven may also forgive you your [own] failings and shortcomings and let them drop (Mark 11:25 AMP).

Declare: If I have *anything* against *anyone*, I'll forgive them — even people who should know better, even those who don't deserve forgiveness — no matter what they did. Because the Bible says there's no one I'm allowed to hold a grudge against. I will just let it drop: leave it, let it go. I'll drop that hurt and pain, and walk away. I will live free.

Read and think about it: Make allowance for each other's faults, and forgive anyone who offends you. Remember, the Lord forgave you, so you must forgive others. Above all, clothe yourselves with love, which binds us all together in perfect harmony (Col. 3:13–14).

Declare: Father, give me the grace to be quick to forgive and slow to get angry. Help me to not speak badly of others. Help me make allowances for each other's faults, and the ability to forgive anyone who offends us. He forgave us, so we can choose to forgive others. Let's clothe ourselves with his love, which binds us all together in perfect harmony.

When People Hurt You

Read and think about it: Faith comes by hearing, and hearing by the Word of God. . . . Let the Word of Christ dwell in you richly (Rom. 10:17, Col. 3:16).

Declare: I understand that forgiveness is a faith proposition, not a feeling. I receive faith to forgive from God's Word. I avail myself to its supernatural help by letting it dwell in me richly, by soaking my spirit in it and continuing to speak it. I won't be surprised when feelings resurface after I've forgiven someone.

Read and think about it: Do not be conformed to this world, but be transformed by the renewing of your mind (Rom. 12:2).

Declare: I understand that feelings have nothing to do with faith. Sometimes it takes a while to renew my mind to forgiveness. I will review and speak the Word — be transformed by the renewing of my

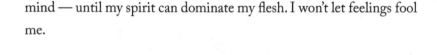

mind — until my spirit can dominate my flesh. I won't let feelings fool me.

....

Read and think about it: For as the heavens are higher than the earth, so are My ways higher than your ways, and My thoughts than your thoughts (Is. 55:9).

Declare: Renewing my mind is changing my thoughts to agree with God's thoughts. I do that by reading his Word because his Word is his will for my life; it's his thoughts. When I study and meditate his thoughts, I replace wrong, worldly thinking with his higher thinking that leads to peace and freedom.

....

Read and think about it: Casting down arguments and every high thing that exalts itself against the knowledge of God, bringing every thought into captivity to the obedience of Christ (2 Cor. 10:5)

Declare: I will replace painful thoughts of hurtful people and events with God's thoughts from his Word. This is how I'm bringing every thought captive to the obedience of Christ. When my mind wanders back to that person or event, I'll double the dose of the Word. I will keep choosing to think on what God has said.

....

Read and think about it: You will keep him in perfect peace, whose mind is stayed on You, because he trusts in You (Is. 26:3).

Declare: I'm the CEO of my thoughts! I am not a victim of my circumstances. I am able to forgive and leave the pain behind by changing what I'm thinking on. It's a beautiful gift to be able to direct my own thoughts. I will focus on God's Word and keep my mind on him because I trust him. As a result, he will keep me in perfect peace.

Read and think about it: But I say to you, love your enemies, bless those who curse you, do good to those who hate you, and pray for those who spitefully use you and persecute you (Matthew 5:44).

Declare: Even if someone has gone out of their way to hurt me on purpose, I will forgive them. God doesn't want me to suffer any of the pain that comes from unforgiveness. I obey him by choosing forgiveness, which kicks the whole situation into supernatural overdrive. I won't want to muck around in the low land of retaliation, revenge, and grudge-holding. God is working on my behalf!

....

Read and think about it: Father forgive them, for they know not what they do (Luke 23:34).

Declare: I realize that the person who has hurt me may never say they're sorry. Them being sorry (or not) has nothing to do with forgiveness. I don't forgive them because they deserve it; I forgive because Jesus is my example, because it's obedient to God, and because it's the way to freedom for me. By forgiving, I cut the chain and walk away from the pain of the past, and keep my blessing pipe clear.

....

Read and think about it: Do not be deceived, God is not mocked; for whatever a man sows, that he will also reap (Gal. 6:7).

Declare: Forgiveness does not mean that I condone what someone has done to me, or that they are getting away with it. It simply means that I am obeying God and going free. I trust God. He is not a fool; he will deal with the one who has hurt me. When I forgive, I'm turning the person and the situation over God and letting him work.

....

Read and think about it: Never take your own revenge, beloved, but leave room for the wrath of God, for it is written, "Vengeance is Mine, I will repay," says the Lord (Rom. 12:19 NASB).

Declare: I will not seek revenge against someone who has hurt me. It's too hard on my heart, and forgiveness is how I guard my heart. I trust God to take care of the situation. My part is to forgive and walk away free.

....

Read and think about it: If it is possible, as much as depends on you, live peaceably with all people (Rom. 12:18).

Declare: When I forgive someone, it doesn't mean I have to trust them ever again. Forgiveness is what I'm commanded to do, but trust must be earned. I will do *my* best to repair broken trust or restore relationship, but I can't force anyone else to repent, change, or live peaceably with me. If I'm in danger physically, emotionally, or any other way, I will set appropriate boundaries to protect myself and those I'm responsible for.

....

Read and think about it: I urge you, brethren, note those who cause divisions and offenses . . . and avoid them (Rom. 16:17).

Declare: Forgiveness does not mean I have to allow a person who's hurt me to have full access into my life. Restoration and trust are possible, but only if behaviors change. That person may not get back all the privileges of relationship. If they are intent on continuing to cause divisions and offense, I will seek the Lord and ask him if it's better for me to separate myself. All I have to do is forgive so that my heart is free.

....

Read and think about it: Moreover if your brother sins against you, go and tell him his fault between you and him alone. If he hears you, you have gained your brother. But if he will not hear, take with you one or two more, that "by the mouth of two or three witnesses every word may be established." And if he refuses to hear them, tell it to the church. But if he refuses even to hear the church, let him be to you like a heathen and a tax collector (Matt. 18:15–17).

Declare: Sometimes I need to confront someone face-to-face in order to forgive or apologize, and sometimes I don't. Only the Lord knows what's required of me in each situation, so I will ask him. If he prompts me to confront, I will step out in faith and obedience and do it, following the Bible instructions above. I trust that he will be there to help, and I believe it will turn out better than I even expect.

....

Read and think about it: Lord, how often shall my brother sin against me, and I forgive him? Up to seven times? . . . I do not say to you, up to seven times, but up to seventy times seven (Matt. 18:21–22).

Declare: I realize that there are times that I might have to forgive someone multiple times — even in the same day. I choose to forgive every time because God *never* wants me to be in bondage to unforgiveness. As I tend to matters of the heart and do things God's way by forgiving, I believe he is working in my situation. I expect a supernatural outcome. No matter how many times I have to forgive in a day, it's always the right thing to do — it always brings God into the situation, and it always brings freedom in my life.

....

Read and think about it: A new commandment I give to you, that you love one another; as I have loved you, that you also love one another (John 13:34).

Declare: There will always come a time when someone disagrees with me or hurts me, so I am going to have to spend my whole life forgiving. I might as well get good at it. Jesus showed me how that's possible, by loving people as he has loved me: unconditionally. I can only do it when I yield to his love that's in me.

....

Read and think about it: Love endures long and is patient and kind. Love never is envious nor boils over with jealousy, is not boastful or vainglorious, does not display itself haughtily. It is not conceited (arrogant and inflated with pride); it is not rude (unmannerly) and does not act unbecomingly. Love (God's love in us) does not insist on its own rights or its own way, for it is not self-seeking; it is not touchy or fretful or resentful; it takes no account of the evil done to it [it pays no attention to a suffered wrong]. It does not rejoice at injustice and unrighteousness, but rejoices when right and truth prevail. Love bears up under anything and everything that comes, is ever ready to believe the best of every person, its hopes are fadeless under all circumstances, and it endures everything [without weakening]. Love never fails (1 Cor. 13:4–8 AMPC).

Declare: This is how God loves me, so it's how I can love others. I choose to walk this out this kind of love every day. I will be patient and kind to everyone, whether they deserve it or not. I won't insist on having things my own way. I won't be touchy or fretful or pay any attention at all when someone does me wrong. I will walk on the victory side of life every single day.

Setting the Captive Free

Read and think about it: Our Father which art in heaven, Hallowed be thy name. Thy kingdom come, Thy will be done in earth, as it is in heaven. Give us this day our daily bread. And forgive us our debts, as we forgive our debtors (Matt. 6:9–12 KJV).

Declare: The same way I forgive, that's how I will be forgiven. I want to be forgiven when I make mistakes, so I will forgive others when they make mistakes. I want to be forgiven quickly, so I will forgive quickly. I want all the mercy I can get, so I will be merciful to others.

··

Read and think about it: Then his master, after he had called him, said to him, "You wicked servant! I forgave you all that debt because you begged me. Should you not also have had compassion on your fellow servant, just as I had pity on you?" And his master was angry, and delivered him to the torturers until he should pay all that was due to him. So My heavenly Father also will do to you if each of you, from his heart, does not forgive his brother his trespasses (Matt. 18:23–35).

Declare: In this Bible story, the wicked servant represents me. I was forgiven everything by my King when I didn't deserve it. So I will have compassion on my fellow humans just as he had compassion on me. I have no right to hold anything against anyone, since I have been forgiven everything. So I will forgive others, and as an added benefit, that can also set them free.

Read and think about it: Offense is sure to come (Luke 17:1).

Declare: I'm going to have to be vigilant about forgiveness all my life. There will always be people to forgive. Offense and hurt are sure to come. It's inevitable! There are opportunities every single day to forgive someone, so I will get good at it.

When They Hurt Someone You Love

Read and think about it: He does not punish us as we deserve or repay us according to our sins and wrongs (Ps. 103:10 GNT).

Declare: When someone hurts people that I care about, I have a choice to make. I can choose mercy, as God does, or judgement. I can't change the past, I can't control what other people do, but I *can* control my response. I can leave the hurts and anger of the past behind when I choose to forgive. God doesn't give me what I deserve or repay me according to my failures, so I won't do that with anyone else.

······························

Read and think about it: For Christ also suffered once for sins, the just for the unjust, that he might bring us to God (1 Pet. 3:18).

Declare: When someone hurts anyone I care about, and I want to say, "Someone has to pay" I'll remember that Jesus already paid for my sin and for the sin of those who have hurt me and my loved ones. Instead of wanting them to feel the same pain that they've caused, I will remember that there's no more payment for sin. It's all done. I'm in covenant with Jesus, and that means I don't live in a kingdom of paybacks; I live in a kingdom of mercy and grace. It's what we've all received.

....

Read and think about it: The thief does not come except to steal, and to kill, and to destroy. I have come that they may have life, and that they may have it more abundantly (John 10:10).

Declare: I will not become collateral damage by harboring unforgiveness on the behalf of others. When the devil works to steal, kill and destroy in someone else's life, I will consider that there are two sides to every story, and I won't believe the worst about something I've only heard. I won't define someone by their worst moments. I'll be quick to forgive and give people the benefit of the doubt.

....

Read and think about it: What a shame—yes, how stupid!—to decide before knowing the facts! (Proverbs 18:13 TLB).

Declare: I won't be stupid by jumping into Mama Bear mode when someone hurts my children. I'll do some investigating and find out what really happening. I won't give my children the idea that they can do no wrong. I'll help them learn about the power of forgiveness and how to resolve conflict on their own so they will depend more on God than on me.

....

Read and think about it: And you shall know the truth, and the truth shall make you free (John 8:32).

Declare: When I don't feel like forgiving someone who has hurt my loved ones, I will just agree with the truth of God's Word. I'll pray things like, "Lord, you want good for _____ and I thank you for that" or "Lord, you are a God of restoration and that is what you desire for _____." I'll agree with the Lord's heart for the person who has hurt my loved one. The Word is alive and powerful. It supernaturally changes hearts. Truth always sets us free. It always wins.

....

Read and think about it: If we walk in the light as He is in the light, we have fellowship with one another, and the blood of Jesus Christ His Son cleanses us from all sin (1 John 1:7).

Declare: God sees the person who has hurt me as his child. He sees that person the same way he sees me! Jesus paid for them with his blood — their sins and their past can be just as wiped out as mine has been. This person has a bright future just like I do! So I will pray for them and for their future.

Forgiveness and Physical Healing

Read and think about it: Bless the LORD, O my soul, and forget not all His benefits: who forgives all your iniquities, who heals all your disease (Ps. 103:2–3).

Declare: Two of God's benefits are forgiveness of our iniquities *and* healing of our sicknesses. Forgiveness and healing go together. That means that when I choose to forgive, I can receive not only emotional and spiritual healing, but I can receive physical healing as well. I won't let unforgiveness hinder my healing. I will check my heart on a regular basis.

Read and think about it: He Himself took our infirmities and bore our sicknesses . . . by whose stripes you were healed (Matt. 8:17, 1 Pet. 2:24).

Declare: It's always God's will to heal me. In his mind, my healing was bought and paid for on the cross over 2,000 years ago. It's a done deal. But unforgiveness is out of God's will. If I'm holding a grudge, I've clogged my blessing pipe and I could be out of position to receive all my benefits in Christ. If God starts to prick my heart about forgiving, I will obey and forgive, because he may be trying to get me into position for physical healing.

Read and think about it: "Which is easier, to say to the paralytic, 'Your sins are forgiven you,' or to say, 'Arise, take up your bed and walk'? But that you may know that the Son of Man has power on earth to forgive sins"—He said to the paralytic, "I say to you, arise, take up your bed, and go to your house" (Mark 2:9–11).

Declare: Jesus has bought and paid for my forgiveness and my healing. I believe and receive both. I walk in his forgiveness and in his healing. My choice to forgive is simply putting God's Word above my emotions and deciding to say, "I forgive." The faster I do that, the better. Instead of rehearsing thoughts of the hurt over and over, I'll just do what God has commanded right away and forgive. That will keep this anointing — his power — flowing into my life in every area, including healing.

Read and think about it: The Spirit of the LORD is upon Me, because He has anointed Me to preach the gospel to the poor; He has sent Me to heal the brokenhearted, to proclaim liberty to the captives and recovery of sight to the blind, to set at liberty those who are oppressed (Luke 4:18).

Declare: Jesus showed us that the power to forgive is the same power that heals. It's supernatural power! The Bible calls that power "anointing." That same spiritual force to preach, heal, and proclaim liberty is also the power behind forgiveness. So if I don't forgive, I could be blocking God's healing anointing and keeping it from working in my life. I know I don't want to do that! So I will forgive.

Especially for Ministers

Read and think about it: And whatever you do in word or deed, do all in the name of the Lord Jesus, giving thanks to God the Father through Him. . . . And whatever you do, do it heartily, as to the Lord and not to men (Col. 3:17, 23).

Declare: If I'm working hard in ministry (or in everyday life) but people don't like it or appreciate it, I'm still okay, because I'm only aiming to please and obey God. Today I'll do everything in the name of Jesus. I'll do it heartily as if I'm doing it only for God and not for anyone else. And I'll be thankful. That will help me avoid the pain of feeling unappreciated. I'll walk in a place of perpetual forgiveness, with all the blessings flowing.

....

Read and think about it: You shall love the LORD your God with all your heart, with all your soul, and with all your mind (Matt. 22:37).

Declare: In this verse, Jesus has given me the recipe for success in ministry. Now I live for an audience of One, and life is sweet. I'm able to forgive people quickly and move on. I'm free to keep my eyes on Jesus and my calling. I will remember to check my heart once in a while and ask myself, "Am I doing what I do for approval? For fame? For money or any reason other than pleasing God?" If the answer is yes, I'll make the adjustment and remember that I do what I do only to please God.

....

Read and think about it: See to it that no one fails to obtain the grace of God; that no "root of bitterness" springs up and causes trouble, and by it many become defiled (Heb. 12:15 ESV).

Declare: One of the most important keys to my success and longevity in ministry is that I keep from getting bitter. And the only way to do that is to forgive quickly and easily, even when someone does me wrong or doesn't appreciate me. So I will forgive! I won't let a root of bitterness spring up in my life. This will keep God's blessings flowing to me.

....

Read and think about it: Let all bitterness, wrath, anger, clamor, and evil speaking be put away from you (Eph. 4:31).

Declare: God put this verse in the Bible because he knew there would be opportunities in my life for bitterness, wrath, anger and evil speaking. So I won't fall for it! I'll obey the Word and keep bitterness at bay by forgiving people quickly. This leads to a life of freedom and empowerment.

....

Read and think about it: But I say to you that for every idle word men may speak, they will give account of it in the day of judgment (Matt. 12:36).

Declare: It's so important that I keep my heart *and my words* right, so that I can stand before God one day and hear "Well done, good and faithful servant." I may not have it in me to serve in ministry, but God has it in him, so I do it for him, with his strength. I vigilantly watch my heart and my words. I will let no corrupt word come out of my mouth, but only speak what edifies the hearers (Eph. 4:29).

....

Read and think about it: Yes, and all who desire to live godly in Christ Jesus will suffer persecution (2 Tim. 3:12).

Declare: I can't be surprised when persecution comes, because the Bible warns me about it. But I can walk victoriously through the trials and hard times! In John 16:33 Jesus tells me, "In the world you will have tribulation; but be of good cheer, I have overcome the world." When I lean on God and forgive, he is faithful to give me encouragement and strength in my weakness. In him I can overcome!

Forgiving Yourself

Read and think about it: There is therefore now no condemnation to those who are in Christ Jesus (Rom. 8:1).

Declare: Forgiving myself is a part of God's plan to keep me free. No one is perfect and every person has blown it at one time or another. That doesn't mean I'm destined to pay for my mistake forever. I'm not disqualified. I am forgiven. The Bible gives many examples of second chances. There is no condemnation to me since I'm in Christ Jesus. I forgive myself.

······················

Read and think about it: God, who is rich in mercy, because of His great love with which He loved us (Eph. 2:4).

Declare: My Heavenly Father is rich in mercy, not judgement. He loves my greatly and is more than willing to give me another chance. The devil would love to keep me in bondage to my past sins, but legally, he doesn't have a leg to stand on. He won't let him keep me thinking about what I've done, feeling guilty or unworthy. Instead I will keep praying faith prayers, walking out God's plan for my life, and helping others. I won't play my guilt in a loop in my head day after day. I receive his forgiveness, in Jesus' name.

....

Read and think about it: If we confess our sins, He is faithful and just to forgive us our sins and to cleanse us from all unrighteousness (1 John 1:9).

Declare: Thank you, Father, that you have made provision for when I goof up. I confess that I sinned. Please forgive me and cleanse me from the propensity to sin again. Thank you for your faithfulness! This forgiveness I receive from You is not based on me and what you've done, it's based on You and your faithfulness. I receive your forgiveness, in Jesus name.

....

Read and think about it: It was God (personally present) in Christ, reconciling and restoring the world to favor with Himself, not counting up and holding against [men] their trespasses [but cancelling them]; and committing to us the message of reconciliation — of the restoration to favor (2 Cor. 5:19 AMPC).

Declare: God has forgiven me. It's that simple. I can't earn or deserve this forgiveness. I received it when I received Christ as my Savior. It's already a done deal, not based on what I've done or haven't done, but based on what Jesus did for me. God is not mad at me. He's already forgiven me, so I forgive myself. I believe and accept his forgiveness.

....

Read and think about it: I write to you, little children, because your sins are forgiven you for His name's sake (1 John 2:12).

Declare: No matter what I've done, God's already forgiven me for his Name's sake. And he loves me. I am assured that forgiving me was God's idea. I believe it, I thank him for it, and I forgive myself. Jesus Christ already paid the price for all my sins, and God is no longer holding any sin against me. I am forgiven.

....

Read and think about it: As far as the east is from the west, so far has He removed our transgressions from us (Ps. 103:12).

Declare: God isn't keeping track of my mistakes and transgressions. There *is* a North pole and a South pole by which to measure the earth, but there are no points from which to measure East from West, so there's no way of measuring how far they are apart. And that's exactly God's point. He has removed my transgressions so far from me that there's no way to measure them. He has made sure there's no way of keeping track of my transgressions. They're gone. He forgives me, so I forgive myself.

....

Read and think about it: This is the covenant that I will make with them after those days, says the LORD: I will put My laws into their hearts, and in their minds I will write them . . . their sins and their lawless deeds I will remember no more (Heb. 10:16–17).

Declare: This is the covenant that I am walking in today because I have accepted Jesus as my Savior. God wrote his law right on my heart and in my mind. He's that close to me. And he says he simply will not remember my sin and trespasses. So I will see myself as God does — without sin. Blameless and pure in his sight.

....

Read and think about it: One thing I do, forgetting those things which are behind and reaching forward to those things which are ahead, I press toward the goal for the prize of the upward call of God in Christ Jesus (Phil. 3:13–14).

Declare: If the apostle Paul did it, I can do it. I can move on from the wrong that I've done. I determine to obey the Bible and forget those things which are behind and reach forward toward God's goal for my life. Everyone has made mistakes and wrong decisions. I won't beat myself up over it any longer.

Read and think about it: Do not rejoice over me, my enemy; when I fall, I will arise (Micah 7:8).

Declare: Everyone is going to trip up or fall down. God is telling me to get up one more time than I fall down. I'm only defeated when I give up. It might take a while, but I can count on God. He knows exactly how to help me get back on track and put things back together, even if other people were involved. He is the God of the second chance.

Read and think about it: Likewise you also, reckon yourselves to be dead indeed to sin, but alive to God in Christ Jesus our Lord. . . . For sin shall not have dominion over you, for you are not under law but under grace (Rom. 6:11, 14).

Declare: I reckon myself dead to sin and alive to God, and sin has no more dominion over me! I forgive myself and will continue to press into God through his Word. I will change my thoughts from what the devil has been telling me (condemnation and shame, rehearsing my failure and what I deserve as a result) to what God is telling me (I'm righteous, beloved, and forgiven in Christ). In Jesus, there is always hope, always another chance. I am forgiven!

So Many Opportunities to Forgive!

Read and think about it: The little foxes . . . spoil the vines (Song 2:15).

Declare: There are a lot of opportunities every day to be irritated, get mad, get even, or hold a grudge. It's not always the big things but the little annoyances that can get me reacting in the flesh, steal my peace, and possibly clog my blessing pipe. I will endeavor to get so good at quickly and easily forgiving that I won't even notice those things. I want to live a lifestyle of forgiveness.

·······························

Read and think about it: (Love) takes no account of the evil done to it [it pays no attention to a suffered wrong] (1 Cor. 13:5 AMPC).

Declare: I believe it's possible to be a doer of this verse. When someone does something to hurt me or make me mad, I will endeavor to take no notice of it, to pay no attention to it. When someone offends me (intentionally or not), I'll forgive automatically before offense even has a chance to hit my heart or get stuck in my mind.

....

Read and think about it: The love of God has been poured out in our hearts by the Holy Spirit who was given to us (Rom. 5:5).

Declare: I can live a lifestyle of forgiveness because God's love is in my heart. This is not a natural human love — not an ooey-gooey feeling — but the supernatural God-kind of love, and it's already in me. I make a choice every day to yield to it.

....

Read and think about it: You shall love your neighbor as yourself (Matt. 19:19).

Declare: When my neighbor irritates me or does me wrong, I won't get mad about it, I'll be quick to forgive them. I will love them by yielding to God's love in my heart. I believe that forgiving them will make me a better witness to them and also enable God to move in the situation.

....

Read and think about it: Real wisdom, God's wisdom, begins with a holy life and is characterized by getting along with others. It is gentle and reasonable, overflowing with mercy and blessings, not hot one day and cold the next (James 3:17 MSG).

Declare: Father, give me your wisdom to get along with those closest to me. Help me to be gentle and reasonable, overflowing with mercy and blessings, not hot one day and cold the next. I won't hold onto irritations, offenses, hurts, or disappointments against them but will aim for peace in our household by forgiving them quickly every time, in Jesus' name.

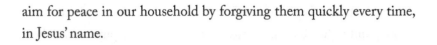

Read and think about it: Therefore let us pursue the things which make for peace and the things by which one may edify another (Rom. 14:19).

Declare: I will pursue the things that make for peace in my family, and will do my best to do things that edify each person, regardless of how well they behave. I won't talk about them or dread their presence. I will forgive them every time and make it possible for God to move in their life. I believe that will also keep my heart at peace and my blessing pipe clear!

Read and think about it: Fools have short fuses and explode all too quickly; the prudent quietly shrug off insults (Prov. 12:16 MSG).

Declare: When someone ignores me or speaks down to me or makes me feel stupid (or any other offensive behavior), I refuse to take it personally or hold a grudge or imagine the worst. I won't explode or meditate on it. I will shrug it off — I'll forgive them, quickly and easily, every time. Forgiveness lets me walk away and forget it, not letting the pain or irritation stick to me.

Read and think about it: For our light affliction, which is but for a moment, is working for us a far more exceeding and eternal weight of glory, while we do not look at the things which are seen, but at the things which are not seen. For the things which are seen are temporary, but the things which are not seen are eternal (2 Corinthians 4: 17–18).

Declare: I refuse to feel sorry for myself. When someone hurts my feelings or irritates me, I won't focus on what I see or feel, I'll focus on

God's truth and forgive them. Everyone has been hurt or betrayed at some point in life, but I'm not going to get into self-pity and let those moments define me. I'm going to rise up, forgive, and put it behind me. I'm the one who forgives, quickly and easily! I'm the one who gets into the Word, puts my shoulders back and my head up, and determines to put the past behind and move forward.

STEP 3

Do This

Now that you've read the stories and meditated and spoken the Word of God over your own life, it's time to do the actual forgiving. Here's where you write down the name(s) of the person you need to forgive and date it. There are two reasons for doing this: first, it's your declaration that you've chosen to forgive — there's something about writing it down that solidifies and finalizes your decision. Second, this is the place you can return to when the feelings come back or when the enemy torments you and says you haven't forgiven. You can point to this page and say, "No you don't, devil. I forgave on this date, in Jesus' name. It's done." Then return to step 2 as often as needed (or the next time you get hurt).

Pray This >>

"Father, thank you for forgiving me and giving me the grace, strength, and faith to forgive others.

On this day, _____, I forgive_____.

I release the pain, and let your peace flood my heart. Thank you that I am now free to move on and live my life full of your blessings and benefits! I trust you. In Jesus' Name, amen."

For the Future, If Needed >>

On this day, _____, I forgive_____.

On this day, _____, I forgive_____.

On this day, _____, I forgive_____.

On this day, _____, I forgive_____.

On this day, _____, I forgive_____.

On this day, _____, I forgive_____.

Receive Jesus as Your Lord and Savior

Asking Jesus to be your Savior is the most important decision you'll ever make. I want to invite you into a relationship with him. It's the starting point for getting your life on the right track. You can't understand any of the principles in the Bible, or in this book, until you've started a relationship with Jesus by asking him into your heart.

There came a time in my life when I had to make a decision to receive Jesus, just like anyone who is a Christian has had to do. I can sincerely say that if it wasn't for him being in my life, I wouldn't be where I am today.

We all are born into sin, according to Romans 3:23: "For everyone has sinned; we all fall short of God's glorious standard" (NLT). Sin separates you, me — everyone — from God.

But 2,000 years ago God sent Jesus, his only Son, to the earth as a man to die on the cross and bear the consequences of our sin, so we could be restored to a perfect relationship, or "right standing," with God: He himself bore our sins in his body on the cross, so that we might die to sins and live for righteousness (1 Pet. 2:24 NIV)

Jesus traded places with us. He actually became sin so that we could become righteous in God's eyes: God made him who had no sin to be sin for us, so that in him we might become the righteousness of God (2 Cor. 5:21 NIV)

God loves you, not because you've done everything right or because you're good, but because *He* is good. He loves you so much that he sent Jesus to pay a price for you that you could never pay. He did this because He wants to have a one-on-one, day-by-day, personal relationship with you.

It is God's will for you to be saved. It's the first step in his plan for your life. If you've never received Jesus as your Savior, then you've never received the benefits of what he did for you on the cross. You are still in a sinful state. You're not yet in a position to receive his help for making the decisions of your life.

But you can receive him *today*. It's not hard.

The Bible says that "if you confess with your mouth the Lord Jesus and believe in your heart that God has raised him from the dead, you will be saved" (Rom. 10:9). All God's blessings and benefits of salvation can be yours if you receive him into your heart.

Jesus died for you, but it's your decision —the most important decision of our life — to invite him into your life.

Think of it like a guy jumping out of a plane with a parachute. Everything goes fine for a while, but unless he makes the decision to pull the rip cord, things are going to turn out badly for him. I encourage you today to pull the cord! You can do it by praying this prayer:

Dear God, I come to You admitting that I am a sinner. I believe that Your Son, Jesus, died on the cross to take away my sin. I also believe he rose from the dead so I can be justified and made righteous through faith in him. Jesus, I receive your sacrifice for me, and I choose to follow You. I ask that You fill me with the power of the Holy Spirit. Thank You for saving me! Amen.

Congratulations, and welcome to the family of God! If you prayed that prayer for the first time, I'd like to hear from you so I can send you a special gift. Please contact me through my website listed on the "About the Author" page. I also encourage you to get into a good Bible-believing church so you can learn more about your faith and grow in your relationship with God.

Notes

1. Lorie Johnson, "The Deadly Consequences of Unforgiveness." *CBN News* (June 2015): https://www.cbn.com/cbnnews/health-science/2015/June/The-Deadly-Consequences-of-Unforgiveness.

2. Ichiro Kawachi, David Sparrow, Avron Spiro, Pantel Vokonas, and Scott T. Weiss, "A Prospective Study of Anger and Coronary Heart Disease: The Normative Aging Study," *Circulation* (Nov. 1996): http://circ.ahajournals.org/content/94/9/2090.full.

3. Cassie Shortsleeve, "Bottled-up anger, anxiety can hurt your heart," *Men's Health on NBCNews.com* (Jan. 2013): http://www.nbcnews.com/id/50629972.

4. Jacqueline Howard, "Watch What Really Happens When Toddlers See You Angry," *The Huffington Post* (Oct. 2014): http://www.huffingtonpost.com/2014/10/10/toddlers-angry-behave-study-video_n_5959482.html.

5. *Science Daily*, "Understanding anger, overcoming anxiety," (Dec. 2012): https://www.sciencedaily.com/releases/2012/12/121204145820.htm.

6. Witvliet C. vanOyen, T.E. Ludwig, and K.L. Vander Laan, "Granting forgiveness or harboring grudges: implications for emotion, physiology, and health," *PubMed.gov.* (March 2001): https://www.ncbi.nlm.nih.gov/pubmed/11340919

7. K.A Lawler, J.W. Younger, R.L. Piferi, et al, "The Unique Effects of Forgiveness on Health: An Exploration of Pathways," *Journal of Behavioral Medicine* (April 2005) 157, doi:10.1007/s10865-005-3665-2.

A Note from the Author

If you liked this book, or it was a blessing to you, please help spread the word!

1) Post about it on social media

2) Write a review online wherever you bought the book.

Thanks!

Karen

About the Author

Karen Jensen Salisbury has been in ministry for about 30 years and a writer for about 40. She and her first husband, Brent, traveled as itinerant ministers and also pioneered two churches in the Northwest.

In 1997, upon Brent's unexpected death, she became senior pastor of their church in Boise, Idaho. She raised their sons, Josh and Ryan, through their teenage years into young men on fire for God.

She was an instructor at Rhema Bible Training College in Broken Arrow, Oklahoma, from 2005 to 2014. In 2014, she married Bob Salisbury, a businessman from Minneapolis. Karen travels and ministers across the U. S. and overseas, sharing what she has learned about the faithfulness of God through good times and bad.

Her teachings and writings have influenced the lives of hundreds of thousands of people all over the world. Her humor, her never-give-up attitude, her love for God, and her strong stand on his Word will bless and inspire you.

Let Karen Encourage You with God's Word

Free To Go On

2-CD series. If you're like most of us, you've had painful things happen to you. But God doesn't want you to stay hurt. Learn how to cut the chains of hurt and live a life of forgiveness.

How to Make the Right Decision Every Time

Book. With biblical wisdom and examples of everyday people, this book will help you learn practical ways to apply God's principles for making decisions.

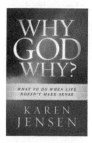

Why God Why

Book. Has something terrible happened in your life? Do you have questions for God? Here is a handbook for getting past the pain.

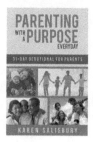

Parenting With a Purpose Every Day

31-day devotional. This is a secret weapon for parents! How to get a vision for your child's life and keep them surrounded with faith by speaking God's Word over them daily.

HOST A PARENTING SEMINAR

 Karen has conducted Parenting With a Purpose Seminars throughout the U.S. and overseas. Her seminars cover both spiritual and practical aspects of parenting for both married and single parents.

Seminar topics include:
- God's plan for your family
- Surrounding your children with faith and love
- Obedience and correction
- Roles and stages of parenting

"This seminar was far above everything I expected. It has equipped me with information that I needed to properly launch my children into their destinies." R.T.

HELP AND ADVICE FOR RAISING YOUR KIDS

These powerful and practical Bible-based lessons have helped families around the world and can equip and encourage any parent, no matter the age of their child.

 CDs or DVDs materials for personal or group use:
- 16 half-hour lessons
- Great for personal use or group study (cell groups, church classes, special meetings, community outreach)
- Workbooks and Group Leader workbook available
- 31 Day devotional for parents

To book a seminar or order materials go to:
www.karenjensensalisbury.org

KAREN
JENSEN
SALISBURY

Go to **www.karenjensensalsibury.org** where you can:

- Contact her personally – she'd love to hear from you

- Book her for speaking engagements

- Shop for Mp3s, CDs, DVDs, books, etc.

- Watch videos of Karen

- Read her blogs "Parenting with Faith" and "This Is the Life"

- Be encouraged by her archived teachings

- Follow her itinerary

- And more . . .

The Harrison House Vision

Proclaiming the truth and the power

Of the Gospel of Jesus Christ

With excellence;

Challenging Christians to

Live victoriously,

Grow spiritually,

Know God intimately.